# RECIDICON

*Reinvent Yourself*

## MALCOLM ALLEN

**RECIDICON II**

Copyright © 2019 by **Malcolm Allen**

**Web: Unconditional.org**

**ISBN:** 9781072328346

.

To all ex-offenders,

you have been given a second chance;

pursue your purpose, and pay it forward.

# Foreword

## A STATE OF MIND:
## MENTAL HEALTH AND RECIDIVISM?

Recidivism refers to the state of being rearrested for repeating a crime even after previously facing the consequences.

As much as recidivism is evident in people without any psychological disorder, it is more common in those with mental illness. About two million people with mental illness are booked into prison every year. Nearly 15% of men and 30% of women who are incarcerated have a serious mental condition. According to reliable studies, there are three times more seriously mentally ill people in jails and prisons than in hospitals in the United States. The reason for this startling reality is the deinstitutionalization of mentally ill people in the middle of the twentieth century; lack of enough community mental health treatment facilities; and the criminalization of mental illness. Many prisons hire a psychiatrist or a psychologist to attend to ill inmates, but still, the challenge has been persistent.

Overall, about 20% of inmates in jails and 15% of inmates in state prisons are estimated to suffer from a mental illness. Considering the total inmate population, this indicates that approximately 383,000 people with a psychiatric disorder were in prison in the United States in 2014, or about ten times the number of patients remaining in state hospitals. Today, about 20% of inmates have an extreme mental illness. This is a worrying prevalence, and the rate has been growing over the years, from 10% in 2006. Pretrial inmates with severe mental disorders are more likely to encounter longer incarcerations than other inmates in many states if they need an evaluation or restoration of competency to stand trial.

A study of state hospital officials in 2015 discovered that 78% or forty states were registering pretrial inmates for medical attention. Mentally ill inmates in some states are reported to spend longer periods waiting for competency restoration so they can be tried than they would spend in prison if convicted of the crime they committed. This shows that having a mental problem while under arrest takes more of their time, as they must go through other procedures first.

It's more disheartening to note that seriously mentally ill offenders have higher rates of recidivism. In many prisons, symptoms of mental illness like schizophrenia, bipolar disorder, depression, psychotic disorder, mania, and post-traumatic disorder, among others, have been reported. While some inmates develop such symptoms in jail, others are confined behind bars with a preexistent mental problem. Most of them don't get proper attention and care, and this could make the illness worse.

Many factors contribute to this illness. For example, lack of employment after an inmate's first release could lead to frustration, forcing them to commit another crime in their search for income. A criminal record mostly makes it difficult for them to get employment or housing. Many ex-prisoners, especially those who have no access to mental health services and support, end up homeless, in emergency rooms, and most of the time, rearrested. An estimated 83% of inmates with a mental illness do not have access to the required treatment. Consequently, their actions result in another arrest, and this leads to depression, anxiety, and other psychological diseases. In severe cases, some inmates suffer from schizoaffective disorder and paranoid schizophrenia. When these mental health problems are left unattended, the recovery process becomes harder as the illness gets more severe. The whole situation becomes more complicated when incarceration or re-arrest worsens what really made them commit a crime.

Lack of support from family and friends after release is another cause. Newly released inmates with a hope for a better life can easily slip into depression if the people close to them fail to offer them support. They end up feeling like they don't belong, or like no one is really concerned about their well-being. Such feelings lead to anxiety and depression, and the condition could worsen into a more complicated issue if they don't get help.

Additionally, victimization of mentally ill inmates by fellow inmates without the illness makes their state severe. It depresses them more. The constant realization that there's something wrong with them makes it even harder for them to cope. Their self-esteem goes down, and self-hatred creeps in. This is a dangerous state because it can greatly contribute to self-harm and suicide.

It's a fact that mentally ill inmates are more likely to commit suicide, which is the number one cause of death in correctional facilities. Studies show that 15–20% of inmates with serious mental illness commit half of all suicides.

Suicides could happen due to isolation. Still, mentally ill inmates are sometimes isolated because of behavioral management issues. Some are exposed to solitary confinement. Such confinement can cause serious psychological problems and even lead to self-harm. The very confinement aimed to help them could result in more tragic outcomes. That's why correctional facilities need the proper resources to handle mentally ill inmates better.

However, getting the necessary resources is a challenge because confining them is expensive. They need more attention and staff, psychiatric medication, and care. In some cases, there are costs incurred while settling or losing lawsuits caused by the treatment of mentally ill inmates. Hence, when people with mental illness are jailed, it's like a financial challenge to the state and local government budgets, as well as correction facilities and the law enforcement system.

But with unity from concerned organizations, there's a solution to this. There should be a community initiative to support treatment for mental, drug, and alcohol problems. Organizations should plan a campaign to reduce the number of mentally ill inmates in prison. This can be done by taking them to hospitals instead of confining them in jail. Furthermore, leaders and mental health professionals should come together to support the treatment of psychologically ill offenders. If they must be in jail, they must have access to medication and support, and later get registered for health coverage.

When a community initiates a project to provide housing, education, and employment to recovering ex-inmates, they won't feel the prick of an unnecessary financial burden. There will be more development, since ex-inmates will now be making a meaningful contribution to the community, instead of draining funds.

# CONTENTS

# INTRODUCTION

**W**hen you yield to that awe-inspiring conviction to never go back, you'll endeavor to grow into the great person you were created to be. No life-changing turnaround happens easily, but the wonderful success that lies ahead is worth it. Let your will to change also give you the determination to overcome every roadblock. As a result, you will burn down everything in your way that causes you to settle for less.

It all starts with acceptance, acknowledging that you made a mistake. Everyone has their shortcomings, and at some point, we've all done something we wished we hadn't. Don't condemn yourself for that one or two times you stumbled and fell. That's what being human means. No one has ever been perfect. Once you understand this, you'll forgive yourself, give yourself a chance to heal and act to clean up your image.

When it comes to recidivism, people who have never been in such a position may condemn you, making you feel like you've committed the worst crime in the world. Since the term "recidivism" means the act of committing an offense even after you've been punished for it, being a victim can spark self-hatred and a sense of worthlessness. The good news is—you don't have to be a victim, at least not after you realize you're so much better than what people think, and what you think about your own self.

Healing starts when you shun negativity and the wrong mindset that comes with it. Self-worth begins in your mind. Knowing there is a great purpose you're meant to fulfill will make you value who you are, and value the ability that's inside of you. When you get your mind to understand you're valuable, you will spring into action. Subsequently, an amazing shift will begin to unfold in your life. You will overcome the proclivities of your past—those tendencies to repeat a mistake. You will no longer be enslaved to unacceptable behavior.

Once you decide to make that change to turn your life around, you'll experience the peace of mind. Thoughts of bad encounters with the law will drift away. The worst possibilities won't race through your mind anymore because deep down, you've purposed to overcome your mistake.

Along with good health, there's nothing more priceless than peace of mind. It means being content with who you are, what you have, and the gifts God has endowed you with. This contentment becomes even more fulfilling when you understand there's a better version of you that will develop if you put forth more effort.

Personal development is a process. After accepting you fell short and paid for your offense, begin to cultivate a free mindset. If you've promised never to go back, you don't owe anyone anything. Not anymore. Your debt has been cleared. You're no longer bound. You've faced the consequences, and now it's your chance to strive to be the best you can be. Your will to become what you were created to be should be stronger than your hesitation to try. Whenever a change is mentioned, our minds rush to imagine how hard it's going to be. If we give in to thoughts of impossibility, we become reluctant to take the first step that would revolutionize our future. Overcoming doubt and hesitation is one crucial move you should achieve before beginning your journey of personal development.

Your new journey will bring a higher quality of life. The flaws that resulted in an undesirable lifestyle will now be out of your way. No more evil intentions, thoughts of defeat, worthlessness, or hopelessness. No more unwanted run-ins with the police. Your days will be brighter than ever. Your health will improve. People will want to interact with the new you. You might even land that job you've been dreaming of. And that automatically elevates your quality of life. It's part of that great shift you will experience just because you were determined to change no matter the odds you had to override.

Instead of allowing the pain to hurt you, make it a tool that prepares you for your destiny. Being prepared for your destiny releases your purpose, which in turn motivates you to pursue your ambitions. The corresponding chapter outlines ways to discover your purpose and live it. Your general outlook will eventually change. That's because you have something to look forward to. The greatness that has been in you since you came to this world will begin to blossom. It will be manifested in what you do and think every day.

Preparation will cause you to work hard to break the cycle of negative habits and wrong thinking patterns. Cutting off a bad cycle can be challenging, and it will require more of your hard work and time. In this chapter, you will learn how to break the cycle of proclivity, and how to maintain your new way of thinking, living, and reacting to situations.

When the wrong cycle is broken, you can only move forward from there. Make up your mind to never look back. Understand that you can't turn back time to erase those instances you committed a crime. Get over the past, regardless of how devastating it was. This chapter will equip you with tips to keep moving even if memories threaten to weigh you down. A few people have experienced relapse along the way, but if you apply the principles detailed in the subsequent chapters, you'll reach the milestone with minimum difficulty. When you're about to give up, there's a motivating principle to renew your inspiration.

An important aspect of moving forward is reviving important family relationships. They may be hesitant at first, but the people who matter most in your life will be your family. This chapter explores the fundamental step of solidifying good family relationships one step at a time. As you build on that, examine your environment—is it the right setting that will support your healing process? Are there factors that might trigger recidivism? If yes, find help from your family to make this important change.

They should also assist you in finding a treatment program if you need one. Such a program is necessary if you've struggled with a mental disorder or drug addiction. Seeking help is a bold step that you should take willingly, knowing that the outcome is for your good. Additionally, it's commendable to join a program that aims to instill the right social skills, values, principles, and beliefs that focus on psychological and social healing. An in-depth discussion concerning this is highlighted herein.

And lastly, it's only you who can determine your own ending. There have been challenges along the way, but they should only make you stronger. Let people's criticism build you instead of crush you. Look for positivity in each situation. In the end, it's only you who knows the truth—the things you've been through to come this far. No one knows about the long nights, the breakdowns, or the outbursts. Be the one to dictate where your life is going.

As you read on, you will get a deeper insight on how to achieve each milestone that's listed above.

# A Solemn Peace of Mind

P eace is one of the most treasured possessions in the world. It has been sought by everyone, including kings and powerful leaders, since the beginning of time. Regardless of one's social class, age, or financial status, inner peace is a prized possession. You deserve it, and the first thing you should do after stepping into the normal world is search for inner peace.

In your heart, you desire it, but because of how people look at you since you were incarcerated, your mind is always troubled. What happened in jail becomes the source of your sleepless nights. You cry yourself to sleep and sometimes end up enduring nightmares—police chasing after you, fellow inmates taunting you or even assaulting you.

The truth is, nothing and no one can take peace away from you unless you allow them to. If you let your mind dwell on the negativity brought about by your incarceration, you're allowing people and circumstances to take away your peace. They didn't give it to you—so why should they take it away? You have the power to stop them, by shifting your attention to the new person you've decided to become.

Forgiven, loved, healed. That's how God sees you. When people see condemnation, He looks at you through merciful eyes. They see pain; He sees the preparation. They see scars; He sees the incredible healing that's going to take place in your life. Most people will picture you as undeserving; He sees the marvelous promises He's yet to fulfill when you hold on to change and positivity. The moment you start seeing yourself through His eyes, He will quiet your troubled mind: no more disastrous thoughts or perceptions. You have accepted everything you are and everything you have. What you own and the amount of money you have won't matter anymore. You'll begin appreciating yourself. Real happiness will fill you. That's what peace is.

As you find happiness, you'll have to restructure your thoughts to maintain a peaceful state of mind. It's not so easy to suddenly change the thoughts that have been running through your mind for a long time. It can be a tough, painful process, but the results are worth the pain. You can control the way you think. It, however, requires much effort, especially if the wrong mindset had become ingrained in you. It's understandable that you couldn't help it because of your mistake and the consequences that followed. But if you let it greatly affect you, you might have to work harder to turn around your thinking.

Change might be hard, but that doesn't mean it's impossible. Your willingness to make a turnaround will ease the process. The internal drive and determination will help you navigate through the ups and downs of starting a new life. A surefire technique to banish negative thinking is occupying your mind with motivational content, information that evokes the right perspective in you. Read or watch something that causes you to change your outlook on life—in this case, life after incarceration. Filling your mind with the right information will eventually cause you to realize how wrong it is to hold on to negative thinking. Enriching yourself with wisdom causes your worry to turn into hope. You will discover there's a second chance, that all is not lost.

Hope gives you peace. A troubled state of mind goes away. Your thoughts become clear, and you stop becoming tensed up about what the future holds. You may not be perfect, but the prospect of good things that can happen when you act is enough to revive the potential that's in you. And deciding to maximize your potential brings more hope since you know that with time, the situation will turn around in your favor.

In the context of recidivism, finding inner peace requires you to know there might be hurdles along the way. There will come a time when you'll have to let go of some friendships. If you examine some of the friendships you had before incarceration, it's likely that they influenced you to go astray—the people you spend your time with matter. You become like the people you constantly interact with. You may not notice this early enough, but if you stop and review some friendships, you'll want to break them off immediately.

Some friends may have been criminals for the longest time. They somehow managed to dodge jail time, and all the while they influenced you to commit a crime. You were unlucky enough to get arrested, charged, and eventually locked up. Being your loyal friends, they even visited you in jail frequently. You served your term, and when you were released, you were still drawn to this wrong friendship. Perhaps you feared loneliness, isolation, and mockery. So, you continued nurturing misleading friendships. In an unfortunate twist of events, you committed another crime and went to jail again. Once more you served your term as your "friends" visited you, so you'd still like to keep that friendship . . . it's time to stop!

Holding on to destructive friendships robs you of your peace. It's paradoxical how their presence in your life gives you comfort, only for their bad influence to send you back to jail, taking away your joy. It doesn't matter how uncomfortable it will feel to end the wrong friendships. Just do it, and you'll sense weight lift away from you. That weight is the fear you harbored inside trying to escape loneliness, the desperation to have friends even if their ways are unacceptable, and the desire to fit in and get their attention.

You don't need their attention to feel contented. You need proper, genuine friendships that can help you grow. Matter of fact, good friends grow together. They correct each other's mistakes even if it's hurtful at first. They encourage each other to do good and adopt acceptable values. They are not selfish—they don't mislead you just so they can achieve their personal interests. They abide by the right principles. They follow the law. And when they notice you're taking the wrong path, they warn you before you mess up. With genuine friends, it's hard to commit a crime. You won't have a relapse. That's how constructive friendships give you peace.

Another way to get peace is through meditation. It is a proven, successful method of helping you cope with life after imprisonment. Meditation can help prevent withdrawal, depression, anxiety, and other difficulties you might face as a newly released ex-inmate. Enroll in a meditation program. Don't be embarrassed to acknowledge you need help. Once you get cracking, you'll discover how important it is to let go. You will gladly accept moving on when you realize the good things awaiting you on the other side. The other side means your new way of thinking, new friends, new principles, and sometimes, a new environment. In some cases, you might need to relocate, even if it's within your city or state. It's advisable not to move too far from your family. They are the people who will always have your back. You need their support on your journey to normalcy. You need them by your side.

Moreover, participating in artistic activities like music, painting, or theatre acting can improve your self-esteem and confidence. Such activities brighten up your world. They ignite your creativity. That automatically attracts the right people in your life, which means opportunities to make a positive contribution to the community. Art helps you take your mind away from your experience in prison. Worry lessens, creating room for growth. That growth is highly essential as it facilitates your reintegration into society. The feeling of isolation disappears. The sense of belonging comes back. Eventually, you realize you're still important despite your imperfections.

Work hard to bring inner peace to your life. Start by setting boundaries. Stop giving your attention to things that don't matter anymore. Instead, concentrate on your growth as an individual. Quit spending too much time on social media. You might end up envying the flashy life people seem to be living when it's not so. You could even start seeing yourself as a lowlife. To avoid that wrong outlook, limit the amount of time you will spend on social media each day. Invest more of your free time on yourself, to enhance your personal development. And when you log in to social media networks, let your interaction with people be constructive. Follow pages that post motivational content. Such content will go a long way helping you gain knowledge, insight, and wisdom.

Nowadays, one can be prone to cyberbullying or trolling if they're not careful. After everything you've been through before and after your incarceration, you don't deserve cyberbullying. If you have one or more social media accounts, stay safe online. If you really must be active online, be cautious. Don't disclose your personal information and contact details to strangers. If you're not interested and you really don't have time, avoid it altogether. You're making a new start, and everything in your life should be meaningful.

You've gone through a lot of pressure since you crashed with the law. Now that you've been released, it's time to implement some relaxation techniques that you can use to take away the stress. Tension shouldn't bind you anymore. Do everything it takes to get rid of it. Go for long walks, admiring nature while you're at it. Work out to release tension. Listen to uplifting music, try yoga, or go for a swim. Start enjoying your hobbies once more. You will feel calm, rejuvenated, and charged-up for that new start.

Spend weekends with your family. Use this abundant time to reconnect with them. If there's a rift between you and your family, forgive each other. Get the bitterness and resentment off your chest. Peace will begin filling your mind, and you will have accomplished one big goal on your road to recovery.

# THE DEBT HAS BEEN PAID

The next big step is resisting the guilt that might still be clinging to you. It's normal to feel guilty after you've done something you know is wrong. Guilt becomes more profound when you get punished and go through bad things in jail. If you don't resist guilt in time, you will start regretting why you went astray in the first place. You will begin scolding yourself and ultimately lose the peace you've fought so hard for.

You're probably affected by what people said about you the moment you were arrested. You let their mean words pierce you and shred you to pieces. The hurt was so great that the only way to cope with it was to remind yourself how wrong you were to break the law. That constant awareness of your mistake is what made guilt build up in you. And getting the guilt out of your heart can be tough, especially when you've let it torture you for a long time. But that shouldn't discourage you from overcoming it. There are several things you can do to get rid of it completely.

First, don't allow thoughts of guilt to convince you how you deserved all the hardship you endured during your incarceration. You paid for your mistakes, and you don't need to suffer anymore. You didn't deserve that hardship. You were only punished so that you could learn never to repeat the crime again. In fact, your time in jail wasn't a hardship. It was a lesson. A lesson to show you how to react. And a lesson to make you maintain your best behavior even in the toughest situations. If you embrace everything you learned after incarceration, you will gain insight, self-control, and calmness.

It's true that your experience in jail was one of the darkest moments of your life. But if you look for the valuable lessons you learned during that time, you'll be wiser. You'll be amazed at how much knowledge you'll gain. You will stop condemning yourself. After your darkest night, the brightest sun will shine. You will see life in an entirely new perspective. You will realize that you're much more than another person's perception of you. Don't feel victimized because you blundered. Their wrong opinion of you doesn't count. It doesn't change who you were meant to be from the beginning. It doesn't determine your future. Their wrong opinion can only hurt you if you let it. You shouldn't. When you decide never to give people's opinion space, it won't affect you. Its impact is negative, and after all the difficulties you've endured, the last thing you need is negativity.

Next, get rid of that feeling that you're unworthy of positive recognition. You need to be applauded for that great person you're becoming. People used to know you by your mistakes; now let them know you by your greatness. Remember that you're no longer in debt. You've served your jail time, whether it was a forty-eight-hour stint or a one-year term. It could have been fourteen years. All you should know is that you've paid the debt. Greatness develops out of hardship. Every great person has had to beat difficulties to get to where they are now. You were not an exception, and that's a good thing—because if you didn't go through difficulty, you would never become as great as you're going to be.

Thirdly, you need consistency. When that feeling of being indebted to people's approval troubles you, fight it. Resist it. If you're doing the right thing, their approval doesn't matter. Only God's affirmation, along with the effort you're putting in, matters. Every other viewpoint is meaningless unless it's meant to correct you or encourage you. Whenever fear about what the future holds fills you, overcome it. Keep on making your best effort. Walk right through fear if you must.

It's human to be afraid of change. Don't be surprised if fear attacks you when you're just one step away from home. You can't come this far only to give up when you're on the verge of success.

Let your consistency help you sail through moments of fear. Don't put yourself through another hell. Your time in prison was enough. Keep on reminding yourself how courageous and confident you are. Starve fearful thoughts completely. Don't give them a chance. Instead, let strength, bravery, and courage fill you. They will become a part of who you are if you fully embrace them. Eventually, it will be easier to overcome the fear that only pushes you backward. Nurture the values that thrust you forward. Lack of courage and the feeling that you owe people something are major things that prevent your progress. Let them go and nurture what really benefits you. That's how you enhance and quicken your progress.

Guilt makes you unable to enjoy the good things in your life. That feeling of being indebted has the same effect. When you realize this, you will banish guilt out of your heart as quickly as you can. You will let that enslaved mindset out of your system without compromise. People won't influence you, even if you were a part of their gang. Or clique. Don't desire to belong to the wrong group. The fact that you were a part of them got you arrested. You don't want a repetition of the hell you went through. Tell yourself you're no longer bound by destructive friendships. The consequences of your mistakes don't bind you either. You really love yourself, so break away from gangs or cliques. If you stick to them, you will face the consequences twice; or thrice. It might be multiple times if you don't break away in time. And if this pattern continues, you will be in constant debt, still paying for your mistakes. Be brave enough to destroy this pattern, for a chance to enjoy an even better life after jail.

For you to eliminate guilt, you need to adopt loyalty. Don't fail yourself. Keep the promise you made to yourself to never slip back. There are certain values you must embrace to fulfill that promise. And loyalty is one of them. It's hard to be disloyal if you are consistent. Loyalty and consistency go hand in hand. Being loyal means, you hold on to courage even if fear is threatening to bring you down. You are determined to keep your word despite any opposition that might come your way.

When you keep your promise, and wonderful things begin to happen, you will feel good about yourself. You will be grateful for the strength you've gathered to be a changed person. Guilt will go away, perhaps without you realizing it. A very effective way to eliminate guilt is appreciating every good thing about yourself. Your gratitude will overpower guilt. You will discover that your strengths surpass your weaknesses. Work on your weaknesses as you embrace your strengths. They may not completely go away, but they will no longer weigh you down.

Make the most of your abilities. If you're business-oriented, start your own small venture—with support of course—and become your own boss. If you're an eloquent speaker, organize a motivational speech that you can empower your community with. Inspire them to conquer recidivism. Tell them it's possible if they're willing. Don't be afraid to recount your experience behind bars. You never know who needs that kind of reassurance, that they are not alone in it. The moment you give back to the community, you won't feel like you're in debt.

And if you're artistically talented, go for it. Make your way to a studio and record some music. Let it be something inspirational that will motivate you and the people around you. Since you don't mind what people say anymore, keep focus, and do your best. Sing your heart out. An amazing relief will come upon you. Music is therapeutic. It will help lift some weight off you—the weight of guilt, doubt, and any other pressure. Healing takes place when you let all that pressure go. You recover the peace that you had lost. Your mood improves. Your appearance becomes radiant. So, don't hold your musical ability back. It's like therapy, only that in your case, it's free!

# A Chance to Turn Pain into Purpose

Everything unpleasant that happened after you were arrested is bound to cause you pain. You might have done wrong, but your feelings were also hurt. You're convinced that you weren't treated right. Maybe you were assaulted or made to wait for your fate for long hours. Your time was wasted. If there was no delay, you would have used that time to do better things. It hurts you to realize that that time was wasted in jail, as you anxiously waited for your opportunity to be free. As you waited, you lost the drive to transform your life. The enthusiasm that you had somehow disappeared. Pain is still torturing you.

You'd like to get over it, but you're not sure how. There are some things you do to eliminate that undesirable feeling.

First, you should transform that pain into a factor that prepares you for a brighter future. You can do this by not letting it bring bitterness to your heart. Even if someone did something bad to you and made you commit a crime that you didn't really want to, convince yourself to forgive them. Failing to forgive people brings you bitterness. And that bitterness only hurts you. It doesn't hurt the person you failed to forgive. Harboring bad emotions makes it harder for you to enjoy freedom or happiness. Whether that bitterness started before or during your time behind bars, it's not worth your attention anymore.

When the bitterness is gone, happiness will come in, and you'll be ready for a brighter future. Hope for a great future gives you the inspiration to dream again and pursue those dreams. You start becoming ambitious again. Your optimism and enthusiasm come back. You start anticipating good things. That gives you the strength to go on regardless of the negative emotions that affected you. And when you have good expectations, you become interested in doing everything that positively pushes you forward.

There's one effective way to beat pain. Getting into action takes your mind away from the terrible things you experienced. The pain starts drifting away. Your attention will be shifted to the wonderful things the future holds. Since you're enthusiastic about a promising future, you will direct all your energy to make it a reality. The minute you realize how much energy you wasted directing your thoughts to painful experiences, you'll never spend another minute dwelling on hurts. They are long gone and thinking about them only refreshes the pain and bad memories. You must expunge those horrible memories out of your mind if you want to be free of pain. Keeping yourself occupied with positive action greatly helps you to stop reliving bad memories.

While you adopt the right outlook, you'll start finding meaning in your life. You begin to search for your purpose. Discovering your purpose and living it enriches your life with fulfillment and prosperity. It increases your sense of self-worth. It shows you how important you are in this world. There's a special assignment you're meant to accomplish. That's your purpose. No one else is meant to achieve it, except you. Everyone has their own unique purpose. That's why you shouldn't compare yourself to others. Their path isn't the same as yours. They may succeed earlier than you, but that doesn't mean you're late. You're free now, and this is the right time for you to discover the amazing potential you possess.

Start by asking yourself: what am I good at? You may be academically intelligent, artistically talented, or extremely good at sports. A perfect way to discover your potential is finding what your talents are and taking time to develop them. Somehow, you'll find out that you stand out in the area you're best at. You'll always be among the best when you put forth your biggest effort.

Soon you'll be recognized, and prosperity will knock on your door. People will start looking up to you as a mentor and a role model. When they do, make a commitment to help them to improve their talents. Share your knowledge. If they've been in jail before, tell them how you're dealing with pain. Encourage them to fight it and embrace happiness. While you encourage them, your will to completely conquer pain will be stronger.

There's no deterioration when you major on positive energy. Your situation doesn't get worse. It improves. The hurt that used to affect you so strongly will have no more power over you. It goes away when you start directing your energy to the good things that can come out of pain.

One of them is preparation, which makes you eligible for any great task ahead. If you've never experienced pain, you'll find it tough handling the challenges you might face on your journey to success. You become prepared by keeping in mind everything life has taught you, especially after you made a mistake.

You learn how to practice self-control, and how to approach difficult situations in a wiser manner. Regardless of the magnitude of your anger when the worst happened, there's a way you could have controlled it. In any tough situation, if you suppress your anger, it won't make you react in a way that causes you pain afterward. Control your anger instead of letting it control you. You have power over it, just like you have power over your thoughts. If you've been thinking and reacting angrily, redirect that into a calm, controlled reaction. Repress the wrong impulses. In the end, you won't have to endure pain and bitterness that comes as a result of uncontrolled anger.

Most of the time, pain comes when people hurt you. In some cases, you never imagined they would cause you such great hurt. You were wounded where it hurt the most. Maybe you expected your best friend to bail you out, but to your disappointment, the moment they learned you were imprisoned, they distanced themselves from you. They acted like strangers, even blocked you on the phone. You were shocked and hurt at the same time. What a terrible feeling! It made you angry and resentful.

At some point, you even wanted revenge. Maybe you changed your mind when you thought about going back to jail. Or you carried out your revenge, and the consequences made you even more bitter. You got imprisoned again. Your revenge made you a recidivist. Afterward, you hated the very sound of the word. You became too embarrassed to interact with people because of your repeated mistakes.

Along the way, you found out you were wrong, and your bitterness escalated. You became angry at yourself. This anger increased your pain. Distress filled your heart. You stayed up at night analyzing the situation and sometimes crying about it. The pain became worse when you couldn't forgive yourself. You had no idea why you were wallowing in pain. You forgot that as much as you should forgive others, you needed to forgive yourself. Guilt lingered on. Fact is, a guilty conscience will prevent you from finding your purpose. It will stop you from discovering what gives you the greatest fulfillment in life.

Negative emotions like pain, bitterness, resentment, and guilt prevent you from knowing what really makes you happy. They take up the space meant for peace and joy. Whenever you try to find your passion, and these uncool emotions are boiling up inside of you, you feel less enthusiastic about pursuing it. You start doubting if your heart is guiding you correctly. And when doubt clouds up your mind, too many discouraging "what-ifs" spring up in your thoughts. What if I fail? What if someone causes me pain again? Will I be able to forgive them one more time? Well, what if you find a loyal friend who will love you, unconditionally? What if you succeed?

You'd like to maintain happiness and hope again, so do whatever it takes to conquer pain. One of the best things you can do is appreciate all the good qualities about yourself. You will feel happier when you know that pain doesn't define you. It doesn't take away your strengths or talents; neither does it determine how your future will be. Instead, it makes you stronger when you act to overcome it. It makes you dare to discover all your talents so that they can empower you and everyone around you.

You can also fight pain by cheering yourself up in a special way. For example, if possible, you could go for a vacation with one of your family or a close friend. It wouldn't be advisable to go alone at this point in your life—loneliness might bring back negative thoughts or get you stuck on the wrong perspective. You need someone next to you, someone who understands what you've been through; someone who cares enough to support you until the end. You need to see the world through their eyes—unconditional love, loyalty, hope, and a new way of life. Listen to their kind words and advice. Then, you'll no longer doubt your importance. You'll see that you really need to give your best in what you're good at. That means you'll be living your purpose.

When you live your purpose, you stop struggling in life. Tasks which are difficult for other people, sometimes become effortless to you. You focus on what you're best at. Amazingly, you get more work done and even help others achieve their objectives. Those who used to undermine you start seeing you differently. They begin viewing you as a respectable person. If you had low self-esteem, that changes while you continue to assist others. Their admiration and respect boost your self-esteem and self-worth.

If pain affected you adversely, you might find yourself speaking harmful, destructive words, even if you don't really want to. Learn to control your speech. Words are powerful. You've heard the statement that the power of life and death is in your tongue. It's true, so speak positively even when the storm is raging. If you feel it's hard for you, don't say anything at all until you fully convince yourself that words are powerful. They can affect your life negatively if they are destructive. So, every time you speak, don't let the pain of your incarceration make you say hurtful words. Speak about the lessons you learned, and how the entire experience made you a wiser person.

The effort you put into positive speaking determines the level of happiness you'll get afterward. You might have been used to harmful speech back in jail, but you're no longer locked up. You are free now. Don't carry the depressingly devastating negativity that used to torture you in jail. You deserve happiness. You're the only one who has the authority to determine how happy you are; or whether you're happy or not. Other people don't have that authority. Neither do circumstances. Unfavorable or not, circumstances don't have power over you. You're the one who can control how they affect you.

To have that control, you need to put forth great effort to counter thoughts of defeat and hopelessness. You're most vulnerable when you first get out of jail. The first several weeks can be a challenge. That's the time you need to gather strength and be the one in control. Wrong opinions, trends, disapproval, and discrimination won't toss you around if you take control. You'll be the one commanding them out of your way. The moment you decide never to give them a chance, they will flee automatically, because they know you will resist them no matter what kind of force they use. When you resist them, they won't have the chance to cause you pain.

In your endeavor to completely conquer recidivism, you also must put effort into your work. The turmoil you endured back in prison can weigh you down occasionally, slowing you down in your profession. This can lead to poor productivity, which is unacceptable if you really want to move a level higher. You can fight turmoil by searching for new inspiration and attending counseling sessions. Try to be happy despite the anxiety and the confusion you went through in the past. It will be hard at first, but eventually, your mind will soon adjust to this life-changing outlook you're adopting.

In some instances, you'll feel like giving up on happiness, but when you feel that way, remind yourself all the hurdles you've jumped. You can't come this far only to give up now. All that effort can't get lost in the wind. It would feel like you never tried at all. But because you never completely lost faith in yourself, don't let a moment of hopelessness ruin your future happiness. Let it awaken the hope that lies in the depth of your heart. Let that ray of hope be your inspiration to dwell on what makes you happy. Let faith and hope replace the pain and propel you to act in a way that brings sunshine to your days.

That wonderful state of happiness will completely be a part of you if you wholeheartedly let it in. It doesn't matter if you were addicted to pain during your incarceration. All you need to be happy is time and willingness. Be open to change; to new things that remarkably elevate your life. It's true that change might take longer than you want. But when it happens, the timing will be perfect. You will be ready to embrace it happily. There will be no obstacle to stop you because, during the time you struggled to reform, you were able to overcome everything that interrupted your progress. You also gained a sensible perception of life. You stopped seeing yourself through the eyes of other people.

Instead, you discovered that grace has won for you; and after all the hardship you had faced, you can only obtain favor. And now, you can't lose the favor that grace has won for you. You were meant to win, and you should fight to win. Fight discouragement. Fight the tempting lure of dangerous gangs. Fight their money-filled enticements. Resist the tendency of sliding back. Overcome the proclivities of your other past life. You have a new life now, and you should fight to maintain it. You have the power it takes to win. There is a winning element inside of you, and all you need is to speak to it, use its power, and let it conquer the difficulties that brought you pain.

There will be someone waiting to assist you. Remain humble and accept their assistance. Sometimes you can't get over pain alone. You need someone to hold your hand. That assistance will take the heavy burden off you; and only then can you be in a clear state of mind, ready to live your purpose.

After you free yourself from the uncool grip of pain, there will be no limit to the fulfillment and happiness you can get. Pain is what prevents you from enjoying the good things in life. But because it will be completely gone, you'll find delight in the abundance of unfailing love, priceless peace, and endless joy. All this doesn't mean challenges won't arise. They will, but since you've discovered the truth, you won't let anyone or anything cause you distress. No situation will trouble you. Whenever you need to solve something, you will calmly take the required steps without losing your happiness. You will act wisely and seek advice when you're in a dilemma. And because you'll begin making the right decisions, the pain will not attack you, as it's one of the consequences of bad decisions.

As you continue to focus more on positive emotions and great perceptions about yourself, every unpleasant element that brought you pain will automatically fade away. There won't be any more pessimism, negativity, or hatred to feed the pain. You will figure out it's gone much later because you'll be completely engrossed in a new, wonderful way of living. You'll start feeling more fulfilled at the end of each day.

Getting a brilliant sense of fulfillment after you do something well means you're accomplishing your purpose. Your enthusiasm and action make it come alive, in your thoughts and your deeds. Subsequently, your greatness will come to life.

# A Chance to Break the Cycle

**M**oving a step ahead involves never letting your attention waver. Be firm and never be tossed around by situations or other people's doubt. It might be a fact that you've gone back to jail multiple times. This cycle can make people around you doubt if you'll ever be able to reform. If you believe it, you can reform. You can break the cycle. Once you're released, consider your freedom a chance to overcome recidivism. Assure yourself convincingly that you'll never be rearrested.

How do you start? You should first realize that you weren't destined to be a recidivist. You were never meant to be a victim, or in trouble always. Let that truth sink deep into your mind. It doesn't matter what your mind—or other people—tell you. They might say it's hard or even impossible. That's their standpoint, not the truth. The truth is the only thing that can help you break free from recidivism. The truth makes you discover how your life is supposed to be. It shows you the right path to follow. Doubt and hesitation may cloud your mind, but the truth never changes. It always remains, and the moment you accept it, you experience a wonderful change when you follow the correct procedure to end bad tendencies.

The road to breaking the cycle requires time, sacrifice, and hard work. The results will not show immediately, but you will see them faster if you don't hesitate to take the first step. There are certain ways to maintain a new, right manner of thinking and behaving.

Most importantly, your emotional IQ will matter a lot. It plays a big role in controlling your thoughts and actions. That's the only way you can achieve great results. Become willful in your quest for a fresh start. Let the awe-inspiring magic of your will cause a magnificent transformation that will end every wrong pattern, whether it's your deeds or thoughts. A strong will makes you accomplish your goals. Don't wait for anything out of the ordinary to mobilize you. You might wait for a lifetime. Liven up as soon as you're free. The right time is now.

Start by doing your utmost to cut off the cycle of proclivity. Reject every unacceptable behavior that pulled you backward. Don't give your mind a chance to think about it. For example, you can distract yourself by doing something good that takes your attention away from bad habits, tendencies, and thoughts. What you choose to do should be something that you thoroughly enjoy. Even if it's a recreational activity or a hobby, it will go a long way in preventing you from repeatedly committing a crime. Don't underestimate it. Let everything you do count. You are determined to break the wrong tendencies, and every little thing you involve yourself with should help you go a level higher.

Next, examine your surroundings. What's around you that could influence you to do wrong? Do you still have an illegal weapon in your house? Or drugs under your possession? Even if you don't use them anymore, drugs and weapons shouldn't have a place in your house. Their very presence could evoke bad memories and even trigger a relapse. The things you see affect your feelings and reactions. So, although someone might have requested you to keep them for a time, the best thing you'd have done is decline. Someone who really cares about your recovery would never put you in a tough position, asking you to keep weapons or drugs. There should be no trace of them where you live.

Other things you might want to get rid of are photos, taken with the wrong people under bad circumstances. Maybe when those photos were snapped, you and your gang were in a certain secret location, brandishing guns and taking drugs. It might have appeared fun then, but now that you've been punished for it, there's no need to continue gazing at those photos. The sight of them repeatedly could have a far-reaching, depressing effect on you. You may not notice it immediately, but when depression and guilt hit you, you'll try to search for what caused them. And you'll find that the simple things you disregard, like photos of your past life, are the major contributors.

Anything that reminds you of your imprisonment or anything that could tempt you to do wrong should get out of the way. Be careful with everything around you. Instead of reliving jail time memories, refresh your mind with information that guides you on how to move on from where you are.

And as you learn to get your life back, spend more of your time with like-minded people who want to transform their lives wonderfully. They'll show you new ideas you'd never think of if you were alone. As a group, you'll all encourage each other to reach your goals. Good friendship and unity will make you stronger, and help you hold on during a difficult period. While you might be tempted to hang out with your old friends who would badly influence you, remember that the wrong company will hinder you from overcoming your past. When you hold on to wrong gangs, the cycle of recidivism will continue tormenting you, and instead of moving forward, your situation might turn out to be worse than it was at the beginning.

Bad gangs may not be physically present immediately when you get back to society. They might be online as your friends, or phone numbers in your contact list. You'll certainly start using your phone again, and it's likely you'll stumble into those contacts. If they're still involved with gang activity, and not willing to change, delete them permanently from your phone. Don't hesitate to do so. Don't even feel guilty about it. You've come a long way, and no one should pull you back.

Occasionally, you'll have to fight off multiple roadblocks. Whenever you face difficulty, remember that nothing great comes easily. Gather your strength, then endeavor to relentlessly navigate through a network of disapproval, doubt, and other discouraging factors. You will have to keep away from anything or anyone who is a roadblock to your progress. This means you might even have to stop going to some places—those wrong places you used to visit prior to your arrests like the bar, or the club. You certainly wouldn't wish to go back to alcoholism and dangerous partying. When you're not sober, you can be easily influenced to go back to crime. And going back starts the pattern of recidivism once again. Therefore, be strong and completely avoid visiting such places.

Instead, use this chance to go to church and listen to the truth that will transform your life for good.

While you make new friends and interact with them, you don't have to narrate everything you went through if you're not comfortable with it. Simply say your life has changed and you're living it from a whole new, transformed perspective. They will understand you, and they won't interrogate you further. But since it wouldn't be wise to keep bad experiences of the past to yourself, talk to someone you trust about it. It could be a close family member, a friend, or a counselor. Tell them to be discreet, that you want to only confide in them. Once they assure you of confidentiality, let it all out. In case you ever endured nightmares, open about it. Don't feel embarrassed. Your counselor might give you advice on how to stop nightmares, and you'll be glad you didn't keep the problem to yourself.

Having constant nightmares is a cycle of its own that needs to be broken. If it's not broken, it will deprive you of your peace and might make you have a relapse. Nightmares can make you anxious in the daytime and can adversely affect the quality of your life. Guard yourself against this. When you talk to your counselor about bad dreams or nightmares, they'll analyze your past personal experiences, and ask you if anything traumatic happened in jail. This is because your daily experiences affect you greatly. They affect your sleep. For instance, someone who has spent a long time in prison, and has had bad encounters, may be more susceptible to nightmares. It's best to ask for help. Your counselor will ask you to check your anxiety and depression levels since these are two major causes of nightmares.

Additionally, you'll be required to check the negative personality traits you might have developed in jail. They could be alienation or isolation, emotional estrangement, anger, or distrustfulness. Don't let these negative traits become a part of your personality. Start working hard to replace them with good character traits. Be courageous and get the support you need to overcome them. Like stated earlier, you will need both emotional and psychological help.

What people might think when you go to see a psychologist shouldn't bother you at all. They might say you lost your mind since you went to jail. They might regard you with contempt and hurl words of mockery at you. Don't let their words hurt you—they are just words. They can't take away the great future you have ahead if you're focused on your recovery. Stand your ground. You know what you're fighting against. You know you're breaking every bad cycle that doesn't deserve to be in your life.

Regardless of how you used to live before, let your sleeping environment be quiet, cool, and dark—no interruptions from the television, your laptop, or PC. At the same time, adopt a regular sleeping routine, avoiding strong drinks a few hours before bedtime.

The lifestyle you had gotten used to in jail is behind you now. Adjusting to a better lifestyle involves changing everything that wasn't right. That's why your sleeping pattern matters a lot. Along with other habits, changing it to become right is part of breaking the cycle of an unhealthy lifestyle.

If your day was tough, find relief from that stress. Try relaxation techniques, like progressive muscle relaxation, whereby you slowly tense and relax different groups of muscles to reduce tension. Just do the best thing that relaxes you before bedtime. It could be cool music or reading a self-help book, and being at ease before sleeping is an indirect but powerful way of breaking the cycle of recidivism.

It might take time for you to adjust fully. Keep working hard on it. In the meantime, replace every bad tendency with a good one. For example, instead of drinking alcohol when you're stressed up, fix yourself your favorite nonalcoholic drink. Make a delightfully delicious fruit punch. Or a smoothie. Let it be something you're not used to every day. Think of its health benefits as you take it. Along with help from those who care about you, your craving for alcohol will eventually go away.

Then, find out when your bad tendencies mostly occur. Who, or what, provokes you? Can you handle a tough situation if you bump into it without warning? If your answer is no, walk away from such scenarios if you don't have to be there. Sometimes you really must be present even if your anger erupts uncontrollably. It could be an argument with your family. In case you can't walk away, give yourself a moment alone to let your anger subside. Then go back when you know you can face anything that comes up.

Whatever situation you find yourself in, learn to react wisely, even if everything isn't going according to your expectations. Many times, in the past, you might have lost control or have flown into a rage whenever there was a disagreement. Maybe your uncontrolled rage is what made you commit a crime and eventually end up in jail. You tried to apologize later, but the damage had already been done. You were punished. Most likely, you didn't have time to deal with the anger that kept on recurring and putting you in trouble. Your time was spent doing community service, which was part of your punishment. But thankfully, you completed your term and you were set free.

As you walked out of prison, you dreaded what lay ahead. You hadn't dealt with your anger yet. You didn't have the will; neither did you have the time. In fact, your stay in prison worsened your anger. During that time, you got into fights a couple of times. You faced more punishment soon afterward. With time, you became more aware of your weakness because of the unfavorable prison environment. This realization precipitated more guilt in you. You were determined to let go of it, but you hadn't realized that anger was still pulling you down. The good thing is you're free now, and you have the time to manage your anger.

This is the perfect time to sign up for sessions whereby you learn how to control your anger. Take time to learn about conflict resolution. Break the cycle of outbursts caused by uncontrolled rage. Your actions will be wiser, and your new way of handling hard situations will automatically end the cycle of recidivism.

Another encouraging fact is that nowadays, there are publicly or privately funded initiatives that aim for better social change. Take advantage of any supportive facility near you and enroll in educational programs that interest you. Some of these facilities even offer employment opportunities, so don't hesitate to check yourself into a helpful program.

Once you enroll, you will get assistance to ensure smooth re-integration to your community. There are numerous reentry programs you can take part in, for example, horticulture, singing during holidays, or helping when a natural disaster occurs.

Along with helping your community, list your personal objectives when you sign up for an educational program. Let your goals be aligned with what you can do best, and what you value the most. Get supplemental education in the field you choose. When you reignite your passion, you will have a strong source of inspiration despite the trouble you encountered in prison. You won't dare to slip back, knowing your dreams are at stake.

Continue to develop and sharpen your social skills. Make use of those skills, resources, and opportunities. They will enable you to accomplish greater success at work. You will not only have professional knowledge, but you will also know how to deal with colleagues in both formal and informal settings. Such vital knowledge makes your work enjoyable and ensures longevity in your career.

It's also advisable to find a good mentor or join a mentorship program. A mentor is someone who can advise you on important life and career issues. They have more experience than you do, and whenever something challenging comes up, you can count on their guidance. Open your mind and become interested in learning as much as you can from them. In the future, you'll probably be a mentor too.

Recidivism will not disrupt your life again if you concentrate fully on breaking every destructive pattern. Your life will be more purposeful. You and your family won't have to put up with costs related to re-incarceration. That money will be spent on more important things that improve your life.

Be grateful for your new lifestyle and keep holding on to it. You'll discover that each day, you become stronger. Let that be your daily motivation. Maintain your strength and faith, finding inspiration from people who have made it, and listening to the advice they give you. They have probably gone through what you're experiencing right now. They know about the isolation, losing friends, your job, and even money. But somehow, they took a bold step to put an end to the cycle of committing crimes. They had faith; they believed it was possible. Heed to their advice. You will unchain yourself from this cycle, too. And ultimately, you'll be able to stabilize your life, making it better than it has ever been.

# A Chance to Pay It Forward

Paying it forward means extending an act of kindness to others after you've been helped, rather than repaying the person who helped you first.

Being acquainted with the people you're helping shouldn't be of any significance when you decide to carry out this selfless act. As it might turn out, most of the people you'll help along the way will be strangers to you. You'll only have one thing in common—you've all been incarcerated one or more times. And because you wouldn't like to go back, you'll try to keep a clean record. You couldn't do it on your own. You needed assistance. Now, since you've been supported and assisted by people who care about you, it's time to make one more remarkable step and help others.

In the process of helping them, expecting a reward afterward should not determine how committed you are. Help them because you don't want them to make the same mistake you made, the mistake that caused you pain, isolation, and unhappiness. They have obviously experienced the same problems as you, and since you found a way to deal with the problems, you're the one in the best position to assist them.

Maybe you're willing to help, but you have no idea how to do it. The following short stories will give you an idea and inspire you to make a lasting change in someone's life.

All these men/women ran afoul of the law. They changed their lives, and used their experiences to do some good.

## DRUG DEALING

Clark was a nineteen-year-old college dropout when he first got arrested. His arrest came as a result of financial strain in his family. His parents had separated, and his mother could barely afford to support all his needs, let alone hers. Clark started feeling bitter when he compared himself to other students in his college. Most of them were from affluent backgrounds. They never lacked anything. In fact, they had more than enough.

Clark began to feel envious. He wished he could own what his fellow students owned—luxurious cars, posh apartments, trendy clothes, and even extravagant partying. Clark hated the life he was living. He felt like the odd one out. He was a bright student, but he couldn't appreciate that. His attention was focused on climbing a level higher financially. Lack of money troubled Clark day after day. His worry became worse with each passing day.

Finally, he couldn't stand it anymore. He befriended Jack, a twenty-year-old man in his neighborhood. Jack wasn't doing any kind of formal employment, but he seemed to be getting money anyway. He had a car, good housing, and generally, a good life. Clark became interested in Jack's way of finding fast money.

Jack did not hesitate to introduce Clark to his "squad," as he called it. The Squad was a group of four young men whose primary occupation was to supply illegal drugs across the West Coast. Their drug-dealing activities were secret and underground, and they managed to evade the law many times. Whenever the Squad suspected the police might be on their trail, they would put their activities to a stop and even move from one state to another.

Clark saw the danger of the fast, crazy life he had begun to live, but he couldn't give it up. At least, not yet. He was now living in an expensive apartment. He was making lots of money. He even started assisting his mother, although she was suspicious. He somehow convinced her he had found a job. Clark knew what he was doing was wrong. He dreaded the day the police would raid his apartment and arrest him together with the rest of the Squad. He wanted to stop, but the prospect of making more money lured him deeper into drug-dealing activities.

One day, after making lots of money, Clark had a disagreement with Jack. They couldn't agree on how much money each of them would take. They ended up fighting; there was so much commotion that one of the neighbors called the police. Clark was shocked when five minutes later, the police stormed in to find him and Jack exchanging blows. Bruised and injured, they were both handcuffed. The apartment was searched, and the drugs Clark had so carefully stashed in the bedroom were found.

Clark was later charged with assault and possession of drugs. He pleaded guilty and was sentenced to two years in prison. His mother was devastated. She couldn't believe that the son she had raised so well, teaching him what's right, taking him to church, had become a drug dealer. She went to visit him in prison, in tears. But still, she was strong and assured Clark she would support him when he got out.

When Clark saw how depressed his mother had become because of his foolish actions, he was touched. He decided to turn his life around if he got out of prison alive. His mother's wise, encouraging words kept him moving. Nevertheless, prison life was tough—overcrowding, fights, mockery, and even worse, occasional stabbings. Clark vowed never to get himself in a fix. He kept to himself most of the time, meditating and thinking about how he would make his life better. He soon renewed his interest in music. It wasn't long before he started composing songs while still in prison. By the time he was released, Clark had composed thirty songs.

He now knew what to do. He would start a career in music. He would also start a foundation to help young people without jobs. The foundation would support young people with musical talent to earn a good living. With the help of his mother and well-wishers, Clark established the Music-for-Hope Foundation. He became the CEO at the age of twenty-two.

Within six months, more than two hundred young people benefited from the foundation's initiatives. They performed at charity events, churches, marketing events, product launches, and many other events. Some of the young people Clark mentored had been in jail, just like him. They shared experiences and encouraged each other to keep doing right. None of them became a victim of recidivism. Their unity gave them the strength to get back on the right path and maintain their good behavior.

Three years later, Clark is now twenty-five. His mother's unwavering support saved his life, and he's still paying it forward by assisting other young people who have been in the same situation he was in previously. Clark was able to go back to college and finish his studies. He finally learned to appreciate the intelligence he was gifted with. He's now pursuing a master's degree in Fine Arts.

## ROBBERY

The second story is about Zoe. She and her fiancé Adrian lived in an inner-city neighborhood in Chicago, where insecurity was common. Without proper education, Zoe found it difficult to find a job. The little money she was making at her beauty shop just wasn't enough. On the other hand, Adrian had no decent job, either. He was a member of a "hood gang" that terrorized people at night and even carried out muggings at times during the day.

Zoe conspired with Adrian to hide guns in their house. She went on to protect him from arrest whenever the police were doing patrols around the neighborhood. This dangerous lifestyle made Zoe close her beauty shop. She started depending entirely on Adrian. His so-called job became their only source of income. Adrian began coming home with huge amounts of money and other valuable items. He would sell these items and use that money for their upkeep. This went on for a year. By this time, Zoe and Adrian had a seven-month-old son. Adrian loved his son, but that wasn't enough to make him quit his dangerous "job."

He became a highly experienced robber and burglar. Sometimes he stole valuable jewelry worth millions from rich people's houses. At one point, he even killed one of his victims.

Adrian's life was cut short soon afterward. He was shot dead after failing to surrender to the police following an unsuccessful robbery. Consequently, after investigations, Zoe was arrested and charged with conspiracy and illegal possession of weapons.

She was sent to a correctional institution that turned out to be her haven for restoration. Although she was separated from her son for several months, Zoe was glad she accepted the help she got at the institution. During the time she was incarcerated, Zoe joined the prison's art program that aimed to assist members in connecting to the creative part of them, in order to find inner peace and freedom.

She was present during all the classes and concerts, together with theatre performances, where other prisoners and members of the community attended. Zoe also joined the mentorship program for further guidance. She learned behavioral and social skills to help with the new change she was making. Zoe promised never to go back.

When her term at the facility was over, Zoe started her own arts program involving poetry, creative writing, dance, and theatre arts. Her program was able to help young girls and even middle-aged women. Since then, Zoe's initiative has changed the lives of hundreds of women who have been in jail before. They have found a haven after incarceration.

Thanks to the program and the mentorship, Zoe found out she became more insightful and could express herself better. She hopes her program will help reduce recidivism rates in her state and if possible, across the nation. And to her ultimate joy, Zoe at last reunited with her then two-year-old son. Her mother had been taking care of him since her incarceration. As a way of paying it forward, Zoe is now a role model and mentor to other women, young or old. She hopes to share everything she learned at the correctional facility with them. And she's devoted never to let her son follow in the footsteps of his father.

## DRIVING UNDER THE INFLUENCE (DUI)

Third, is the story of Jacob, who had been arrested multiple times before finally deciding to reform. Although his multiple stints in jail were short-lived, Jacob was beginning to lose peace and be less productive at work. His first arrest came as a result of drunk driving. He spent a week in jail before being sent to rehab. Despite his short stay in jail, Jacob had the worst time of his life. He got into an altercation with a fellow inmate. He ended up with a broken arm and was given a warning by the correction officer. What followed next was a two-week stay in rehab. Jacob was somehow able to beat his overconsumption of alcohol. He was released after he successfully completed his rehab program.

His sobriety did not last long, however. A month later, he was arrested again, for driving under the influence of alcohol. Jacob's next stay in jail lasted for nine weeks. His relapse greatly brought his spirits down, and he almost slid into depression. What rescued him was his second stay in rehab and support from his best friend, Brandon. Brandon kept encouraging Jacob to fight alcoholism. Whenever a breakdown was threatening to crush Jacob, Brandon was always by his side. He gave him friendly and inspirational talk. Sometimes he even added humor, to put a smile on Jacob's face.

Brandon's support kept Jacob from getting worse. He got better. And even though he faced one more arrest after that, Jacob was able to change, with Brandon's help. He overcame alcoholism and later quit drinking altogether. Jacob felt indebted to Brandon. He was so thankful for the help, and he spent hours looking for a way to show his gratitude. He couldn't think of anything. Brandon was rich. He had everything he needed—a good job and a loving family. Jacob finally decided to be a loyal friend to Brandon.

Still, he planned to help other people who were struggling with alcoholism. *I will gladly pay it forward,* Jacob decided. He started working with support groups for people battling alcoholism.

He told his story, how he endured tough nights in jail and challenging moments in rehab. Jacob's story gave people hope. He assured them they could beat alcoholism, no matter how grave their addiction was. Although he spoke about his two instances of relapse, Jacob asserted that nothing was impossible if you had faith. His speeches transformed people's lives. He started getting invitations across his state, to speak at meetings aiming at assisting people convicted of DUI. Jacob told the entire truth about the problem of alcoholism. He was lauded for his openness. Soon, he was traveling around the country, speaking about how to overcome alcoholism. Thousands of people were inspired by his speeches. Today, Jacob is still counseling people who have gone through the same predicament he was in.

## DOMESTIC VIOLENCE

Next is the story of Rick, who was a repeat offender for domestic violence. He was a brilliant IT expert, but he had a weakness. He couldn't control his anger. Rick had been married to his wife Lisa for a year. The first several months of their marriage were wonderful. Everything seemed to be going well. Lisa had a promising career as an actress. She and Rick even moved to Los Angeles so that she could establish her career as a Hollywood actress.

Rick was very supportive of Lisa. He understood the nature of her job. He didn't mind when she had to be away for days. He knew she loved him, and all she wanted was to use her talent in the best way she could.

One evening, Lisa came home after a long day on the set of an upcoming movie. Rick was excitedly waiting for her as he had missed her deeply. She was glad to see him, and their five-year-old daughter Lynn.

Lisa was extremely tired, so she went to freshen up for dinner. She left her phone on the living room table as she always did. Lynn, being the bright, curious girl she was, grabbed her mother's phone and started checking its contents. Her attention was soon drawn to the photo gallery. Her mother's appealingly beautiful photos wowed her. Excited and fascinated, Lynn dashed to the lounge where her father was unwinding with a glass of wine. She went to his side.

"Daddy, look how beautiful mom is in these photos!" Rick admired Lisa's photos, and Lynn flipped through them, getting more excited with each photo. Suddenly, she and Rick came across a photo of Lisa kissing a fellow actor. Upon seeing the photo, Rick grabbed the phone from Lynn's hands. "Go and tell mom to hurry up," Rick told his daughter.

Puzzled, Lynn ran upstairs to call her mom. Lisa came to the lounge moments later, wondering why Rick was rushing her yet they weren't going anywhere. When she saw how furious he was, and the way he was holding her phone, Lisa immediately understood what was going on. She was aware of Rick's weakness—uncontrollable anger. She knew she had to act fast before he did something crazy.

"We had to do a photo shoot to promote our latest movie."

Rick shook his head skeptically, not believing a word Lisa said.

"I have no problem with that, but why didn't you tell me in advance?! These photos of you kissing another man took me by surprise. What do you think I'm feeling now?"

Lisa tried to explain she had no idea the photo shoot would come up so soon. Rick interrupted her angrily, smashing her phone on the floor and tossing his glass of wine against the wall.

What followed next was dramatic. Scared, Lynn rushed to her bedroom and wisely, thought of calling her aunt, who lived nearby. In the meantime, Rick was hitting Lisa, claiming how she no longer loved him, that he was not the priority in her life anymore. Lisa tried to fight back, but Rick overpowered her. He left marks on her face, and if Lisa's sister hadn't come in time, Rick would have hurt her further.

Lisa's sister helped her report this instance of domestic violence. She later went to get treatment for her bruises.

Rick was convicted of domestic violence. He was ordered to spend six months in jail. He would also be on probation for three years. Although he later apologized to Lisa for hurting her, it took time for her to forgive him completely. When she finally forgave him, she thought about what really caused the fight. It was partly her fault, she figured. She should have told Rick there was a possibility of such a photo shoot. But then, he had no right to react the way he did. He should have understood everything about her job.

Lisa still loved Rick. Her influential friends helped her bail him out before his term was over. He and Lisa made up, and they went back to being the happy family they once were. Lisa continued getting more roles in blockbuster movies. She became busy and had to be away from Rick for days, again.

One night when Lisa failed to pick up his call, Rick used his knowledge in technology and tracked her location. He found her in a compromising position with another young man, who was also an actor. Rick's anger flared up for the second time. Without warning, he lunged at the young man and knocked him down with a single blow. Then he went for Lisa, who was frozen to the spot, transfixed with astonishment. He slapped her before she could explain, then went on to rain more blows on her. He badly hurt her.

Rick was arrested again and charged with assault and domestic violence. This second offense landed him in jail for two years. He later realized that Lisa and the young man had been rehearsing a movie scene. Rick began regretting why he didn't give Lisa a chance to explain. He apologized again, this time so remorsefully that Lisa could see he was truly sorry. Her love for him was still strong, and she forgave him again. She promised to help him deal with his anger. But before that, Rick had to serve his term in jail.

While incarcerated, he authored a course on Domestic Violence (DV). He wanted to enlighten others on how to deal with domestic issues calmly, without resorting to violence as a solution. Rick couldn't stand the thought of losing his wife and daughter. He signed up for anger management classes. He completed his course a better man, a loving father, and a romantic husband. He even took his family for a vacation in the Bahamas, to make it up to them.

Additionally, Rick continues to pay it forward. He now volunteers for DV organizations and speaks to teens at high schools and colleges.

## CAR THEFT

Leslie was only nineteen when she first broke the law. After failing to join college or university due to family issues, Leslie joined the wrong group of friends. All three of them were about her age. None of them had a job. One of the friends, Frankie, suggested they start the business of car theft as a way of making a lot of money quickly.

The other two were hesitant, but Leslie seemed to like Frankie's idea. She could not think of another way to make money since she wasn't qualified for a good job. Leslie and Frankie moved in together to a cheap apartment near Atlanta. They didn't mind what anyone would say. Their goal was to make money and live a better life. Leslie was now convinced that her family didn't care about her anymore. She stopped communicating with them and dedicated all her time to learn the art of car theft.

Frankie mysteriously managed to find a gun. In a period of eight months, he and Leslie stole six cars. They would later find a way of reselling them. Once they did, they moved to a better house in Atlanta. They used all kinds of methods to steal cars, including carjacking, stealing keys from unsuspecting owners, and using hammers to break locks.

One fateful night, Frankie and Leslie were in the process of carjacking when the police suddenly pounced on them. Frankie tried resisting arrest. An impatient officer shot him, killing him on the spot. Horrified, Leslie surrendered. She later pleaded guilty to charges of car theft and conspiracy. Consequently, she stayed in jail for four years before being released because of good behavior.

Leslie's stay in jail taught her to think twice about her life. She had wasted more than five years of her young life chasing after money. She realized while in prison that money was no longer that important. Her life is what really mattered. A female officer at the prison offered her counseling during the time she was incarcerated until she was released.

Leslie took the advice seriously. It saved her life. She reconciled with her family. They readily forgave her and promised to help her with her future endeavors. Leslie got the support she needed and went to university to study psychology and professional counseling. Today, Leslie, now thirty-two, speaks to young people, advising them to have the right perspective and hang out with the right friends. Leslie is a sought-after motivational speaker and psychologist, who travels across the country, inspiring other young people.

## CONCLUSION

All these stories show how formerly incarcerated people got assistance and took it positively. Although some of them repeated their mistakes, they still believed they would one day overcome. Relapse did not kill their hope of reforming. Instead, it made them push harder until they completely came out victorious.

You, too, can win. There's nothing impossible if you have a strong will and a little faith. If there's no doubt in you, a conviction that you have the power to wonderfully transform your life is all you need. Then, you'll be required to take the right action, with the help of those who are concerned about you. When you successfully become a better person, it will be possible to help others who are in trouble. That's what paying it forward means—you can't repay the person who helped you. You extend that help to those in need. And when you do that, your contribution will outlive you for decades to come.

# A Chance to Write Your Own Ending

D espite the tempestuous turmoil you went through in the past, you must decide never to slip back. Quit re-living horrifying memories in your mind. Instead, focus on good memories, and completely erase bad ones. If you must remember anything, don't dwell on bad events. Bad memories have a depressing effect on you. Turn your attention to something uplifting that could make you aspire to be better than you were before.

For you to move forward, everything unpleasant that happened in jail must get out of your mind. It might seem hard, but it's possible; for instance, when you do a new, exciting thing. Such an activity fascinates you and prevents your thoughts from spinning out of control. It takes all your attention. Therefore, you won't have to persevere the torment of unpleasant memories running through your mind. Examples of things you can do are learn a new sport or artistic activity, visit an art gallery, start dancing lessons, or find a new passion. There are many things you can do, things you can be totally engrossed in anytime. They'll help you heal faster since there will be no room for bad events that you faced in the past.

Every day, live by inspiring principles which encourage you to keep moving. You can find them in books and journals. It's easy to access them nowadays because technology has made it easier. Whether you have a smartphone, tablet, or laptop, you can easily access inspirational material in the form of eBooks or articles. Set aside time each day and read something that uplifts you. Choose what makes you want to embark on self-improvement. Or something that stirs up your creativity. You might be amazed to discover how much there is to learn and develop in order to elevate your life.

Whenever your spirits are down, spend time on good things that make you happy. Try to review your dreams and look back to see how far you've come until now. If you've practiced what's written in the previous chapters, you've achieved something, so celebrate that victory. When you celebrate and reward yourself, your spirits go up again, and you feel stoked up about taking another step forward.

Something important you can't ignore as you move on is your family. There might have been pressure and disagreements when you got locked up, but now it's time to revive your relationship with them and strengthen it. Your family means more than the world to you. Their love is bigger than your mistakes. It's greater than feelings of being forsaken and abandoned. The impact of their love is more far-reaching than those incidents when you argued heatedly about your incarceration. Arguments don't last forever, but love does. So, commit yourself to reestablish that wonderful family relationship.

There are many things you can do to strengthen your family bond. If you all haven't seen each other in a long time, plan a get-together. Enjoy the good time and use this chance to prove to them you're not the same person you used to be. Then, you can participate in a fun activity together. This takes the pressure off you and could prompt you to forgive each other despite what came between you previously. And whenever you can, attend family events like graduations, birthdays, and weddings. Don't wait for a tragedy to bring you together as a family. Treasure the good times more. Let your bond be strengthened by happiness, not sorrow.

When you value your family, and you work to eliminate anything that comes between you, you get more support that assists you to move ahead. You won't feel isolated again because you now have them by your side. They will be there in times of need, and you can confide in them whenever you feel you should let something out. The effects of feeling lonely and isolated won't bother you at all. Loneliness and isolation can cause or worsen depression, but when you have your family by your side, depression will not be a part of you.

They will help you make the right decisions right from the moment you come back home. They won't rush you—they'll understand that you need time to adjust. They'll take care of you when you're most vulnerable, thus eliminating the chances of a relapse. Then when you gain strength, you won't have a reason to look back. Your desire will be to press ahead, knowing that you are valued, that the most important people in your life are concerned about you.

They know what matters to you. Hence, they'll assist you in choosing a path that's best for you. They won't allow you to make a mistake again. That's because their love is unconditional and everlasting.

The crime you committed cannot stop them from caring about your well-being. They understand that no one can boast of perfection—anyone can make a mistake. So, as they help you, don't feel like you're a burden to them. You'll also be of assistance to them in the future, but hopefully, under better circumstances.

As you get all the support you need, visualize yourself making it. Let the word *success* echo in your mind repeatedly. Don't ever let thoughts of failure take over. Teach your mind to visualize success and triumph. An optimistic outlook can give you the energy and strength you need to take every action that pushes you higher. If you ever felt drained because negativity weighed you down, that feeling will disappear and, in its place, there will be energy and optimism.

At times, you might find yourself feeling stressed out, especially before you fully adjust to a new life. Whenever stress attacks you, come up with effective ways to deal with it. You don't have to figure out how all by yourself. Read articles on how to deal with stress. Act and enjoy the results. Or you can ask your family and close friends for help. They'll be impressed by your willingness to heal, and they'll be more than ready to assist you.

Don't forget to look for positivity in everything, even when you face a challenge. Remember that if a problem was meant to break you, it would never have happened. Being arrested didn't break you. Yes, it hurt you, but it didn't tear you apart. Better still, your time in prison didn't crush you. It affected you negatively, but still, that wasn't enough to destroy you. You got out. You're here now. And this is your chance to move forward. Every problem you faced before and after your incarceration made you stronger, wiser, grateful; better. If you weren't arrested, you would never know the success you're capable of achieving. So, consider your arrest as a factor that launched a greater destiny for you. Don't regret that you stepped in jail.

Appreciate that it was all a lesson to teach you what really matters in life.

Set your goals high. Then, don't allow interruptions from bad habits and bad company to prevent you from accomplishing those goals. All you need to do is take action to make your goals a reality. You already know about setting realistic goals, so when you start making moves to achieve them, you won't feel like you have mountains to move. You'll feel a positive force convincing you to reach your goals. You'll chase after your dreams and ambitions even before anything prompts you. Although you'll listen to how others made it, you won't sit back and wait for someone to motivate you. You'll get into action because you wouldn't like to remain in the same state.

No matter what you do, always shift all your attention to your vision and your future. You don't have the ability to change how your past is, but you have the power to dictate how your future will be. Instead of worrying about the coming days, plan. It should be an easy but meaningful one, a simple plan that clearly shows how your new life will be. You'll have a new job that you love, a solid relationship with your family, good friends, reachable goals, and the right perspective on life. In that plan, list every bad thing you should stop doing. Never let your weaknesses pull you down again. Everything you've learned will help you know how to deal with them. Your weaknesses may not go away immediately or completely, but your reaction and your personality will have greatly improved.

While you're dealing with your weaknesses, stop running away from problems. Running will only worsen the situation. In the end, it hurts you. Whether it's an unpaid bill or an apology you owe someone, don't be afraid to face it. Seek the right financial assistance to settle your debts. Those who really understand what you've been through will certainly agree to help you out. And if you need to apologize to someone and renew a good relationship with them, be humble and present your apology. No one can be too heartless to accept a genuine apology. Keep in mind that your humility will make people respect you. Apologizing means you're wise and you are willing to correct your mistake.

Another great step that can help you move forward is when you stop looking for an explanation for everything. Most of the answers you're looking for are related to what happened in the past. Stop looking, because you won't find answers to all those things. Don't give up your peace for something you'll never be able to change. You don't have to know everything. So, stop wasting hours searching for explanations you'll never get. You'll have more peace if you focus on the present and endeavor to make your future brighter.

Meanwhile, identify your fears and let them go. Fear brings torment. You don't need that. You need comfort. You encountered enough trouble. It's time to embrace change. Spoil yourself a bit. At least, do something that makes you smile. Simple things like a short vacation or a road trip can really go a long way. Do anything in your power to cheer yourself up and get rid of fear.

Once fear is gone, you can be confident in yourself and your abilities. Trust you with yourself. Don't put into consideration what people said. If they spoke discouragingly, counteract those negative comments with uplifting affirmations. This will boost your enthusiasm and strengthen your will to keep moving.

Then, plan a favorable schedule that you can follow comfortably. Be serious about sticking to it, but don't be too tough on yourself. In other words, don't overwork yourself. Overworking causes fatigue, which in turn slows you down. Pace yourself. Get enough rest. That way, you'll be more alert and energetic, ready to make yourself more valuable each day.

When you start acting positively, trouble will no longer follow you. It could be surprising how disaster showed up wherever you went when you used to hang out with the wrong gang. But since you cut yourself off from the group, you stopped getting into trouble. Good things began happening when you joined groups that aim to improve the life of every member. In that group, you found friends who were not selfish. They don't handle illegal weapons or drugs, and they would never ask you to hide such dangerous stuff in your house. You can trust their friendship because it will never mislead you again.

Because you've now joined the right group, don't give in to the temptation to go back to your former gang. Even if they boasted that the law would never catch up with them, resist the temptation to answer their calls. Don't even consider the amount of money they'll offer you. You don't know how their story will end. You and your family have dealt with enough trouble. You don't need it anymore.

After you've gotten over everything that used to trouble you, you can be a role model to others who have been re-incarcerated before. Every time you happen to be in a correction facility and someone new checks in, go out of your way to speak to them. Tell them how you're coping with life. Make it clear to them that they shouldn't be afraid of change. They will realize they're not the first ones to be in that situation, and purpose to start fresh. When you know you've helped someone and saved their life, it will give you happiness and a sense of fulfillment.

After all the ups and downs you've trudged through to get here, don't let anyone take away your success. You shouldn't give them a chance to lure you back to crime. They haven't known what it means to be re-incarcerated. They didn't put up with everything undesirable that attacked you upon your arrest. They don't know about your lonely nights, those times you broke down, or those times your reactions went out of control. You are the only one who knows what really happened. The truth, the lies, and the denials remain in your head and in your heart.

That means it's only you who can determine how your future will be. You should, therefore, decide to be the one who controls the direction of your life. First, understand that every difficulty you encountered before, during, and after being incarcerated was supposed to strengthen you. You didn't know how strong you were until you broke the law. Difficulties stirred up amazing strength in you. Yes, you got into trouble a few times, but that didn't break you. You became stronger. Now, use that strength to maintain this new, better life you've found. You got through the worst, so don't allow any more destructive interference in your life.

In the end, your happiness is in your hands. You can choose to be happy with the new course your life is taking, instead of letting resentment stay in your heart. You have the power to be happy even in the middle of a storm. That doesn't mean you should ignore any difficulty you're facing. It means you should correctly solve every problem without letting it steal your happiness. The severity of the problem may be more than you've ever handled. Nevertheless, don't give up on solving it. Seek assistance to solve everything that's troubling you. It's not good to find solutions all by yourself. We all need support. Let the right people help you, whether it's a financial crisis, an addiction, a career challenge, or a psychological problem. The help you get speeds up the healing process because you're not in it alone. Help is one major factor that contributes to a happier life after incarceration.

To make your new life even better, make wise choices that favor you, not those that please people. The choices and decisions you make now will significantly affect your future. Therefore, with every choice, keep your future in mind. It's very important, since your past and all the mistakes in it are gone. Consider the effects of every decision before you jump to it. Is it risky? How will it affect you and the people close to you? If you have doubts about anything, consult your family or friends. They want the best for you, and they'll give you an honest opinion. Although their opinion might disappoint you, think about it carefully before you make a choice. You'll be glad you did when later you discover the effects your decision would have.

Despite your circumstances or environment, don't let them affect your decision-making. Don't allow them to drag you down either. Take the entire responsibility for your life and your choices. Those who used to influence you wrongly before might have pressured you to choose recklessly, but you don't belong to that group anymore. You are different now. You have the authority to dictate how your life will unfold with each new day.

Good decision-making involves knowledge and wisdom. To be wise, get wisdom from books. Every day set aside time to read. Make that effort to be more knowledgeable. Knowledge helps you make wiser decisions. You'll grow personally and be a great help to others.

Next, learn to encourage yourself. Even if you must do it multiple times a day, spend a few minutes alone. Take that time to remind yourself that your best days are yet to come. Affirm how gifted you are, and how you are an inspiration to your community. Be grateful for the wonderful progress you've made so far. Tell yourself that the hardest part is over, and it's now possible to live your fullest life.

Then, examine where you focus most of your attention. Do you often give discouraging statements your attention? How does your approach affect the way you feel? Instead of letting disapproval and discouragement pull you down, let them mobilize you, even to do better than anyone could expect. If you noticed a mistake because someone pointed it out, go ahead to correct it. What you give attention to affects your level of happiness. To avoid sadness, let your attention be focused on how any situation can help you become better, rather than hurt you or stop you from moving on.

While you move on, criticism will be inevitable at some points in your life. Some people will try to find the slightest fault in you. They will criticize your style, your actions, and even your speech. Their criticism shouldn't discourage you. It shouldn't dampen your optimism about the future. Find out what they're criticizing you for. Sometimes it could be true. If it is, correct your mistake. If there's no truth in their criticism, let it pass because they are just jealous of your progress.

The annoying way people sometimes behave can make you irritated. They might be snobbish, contemptuous, or hateful because you once went to jail. That's their nature, so don't let it get on your nerves. Stop trying to control them. Don't force yourself on them either. You don't need their approval if you're doing what's good. If you must deal with such people, especially at work, learn people management skills that will help you understand others and their behaviors.

Don't spend each day of your life trying to live and please or impress people. Live to do what's right. Live to find the greatness you were meant to possess. Live to enjoy the abundance, the peace, and the wondrous riches that come with it.

# E.M.E.R.G.E. System

Getting back your life becomes easier when you draw up a smart strategy for living a wonderful life. In this chapter, the "Emerge System" is precisely described. Highlighted in seven steps, it will give you realistic methods of climbing a step higher in the ladder of success.

## 1. Engage with Mentors

### (Day 1 – 5)

After you get connected to the right mentors, begin your journey with them and involve them fully as you make progress. Avoid hesitation and holding back. Speak out when you're unsure of which direction to take. They have been down this road before and therefore they are in the best position to guide you. Their advice and guidance will prevent you from making a mistake. Thereafter, you will get to your destiny in a shorter period, because mistakes delay your breakthrough. Although you learn from mistakes, it's good to avoid making them. It's even better to learn from the mistakes of others who conquered recidivism before you.

## 2.  Map Your Future

**(Day 6 – 10)**

The future is approaching, and you can't just wait without a vision. Spare a moment and write down your vision for the future. What are your expectations in the days to come? What about five years from now? Will you be able to show how much you have accomplished? What picture comes to mind when you visualize the coming years? You may not be able to answer all these questions at once, but when you make plans and outline how you expect your life to be, you won't dread the coming days.

### 3. Equip Yourself

**(Day 11 – 15)**

There are certain things you need as you reenter the community. Education, communication skills, social skills, and access to basic amenities are essential. You cannot do without them. They empower you to become the best you can be. Fortunately, your community offers these resources, and there are specific ones set aside for people who have been incarcerated at some point in their lives. Equipping yourself with everything you require in order to succeed is one of the first steps you should take after you complete your term.

### 4. Reinvent Yourself

**(Day 16 – 20)**

This means completely changing to become a new person. Your past flaws don't count anymore. They have no more influence over you. This is your beginning, and you're learning new things. The person you used to be before shouldn't be reflected in what you'll become after your reinvention. Moreover, reinvention doesn't mean perfection. It means a transformed, recharged you. You will still have imperfections, but they won't stop you from living a purposeful life. Your transformation will overshadow your weaknesses, and only the best of you will be seen.

## 5. Give Back to Your Community

## (Day 21 – 25)

The perfect way to show your appreciation to the community is to give back. Their assistance has raised you back to your feet, and it's your turn to offer what you can. If you can lend a hand in community development, workshops, seminars, or other projects, do so willingly and cheerfully. You can even volunteer and give them full support without expecting payment in return. Their gratitude alone will boost your willingness to be selfless. With time, your new selfless quality will bring rewards your way. Your family, friends, and the community will want to give more assistance to you in your personal endeavors.

## 6.   Evaluate the Results

**(Day 26 – 30)**

After all the hard work you've put in, give yourself a chance to look back at what you have achieved so far. There are results that have started showing. Some of them may be extremely great, far-reaching enough to shift the direction of your life positively. Others are small but still visible and impactful. Appreciate every positive result you get, whether great or small. Continue putting more work into your personal development. You're still going through a process, and it takes patience, devotion, and time to see life-changing results.

## 7. Live Your Best Life

Everything you've done to facilitate your transformation should greatly improve your life. Be committed to your growth. It should be the most important goal because growth is continuous. Let every new day be an opportunity to improve yourself. As you begin your day, affirm that this is another chance to be better than you were the previous day.

In the course of your advancement, live in alignment with your purpose. Find out what you can start acting on immediately that will enable you to live in accordance with your purpose. Look for ways that can motivate you to live true to your purpose within every circumstance you might be in, every moment of the day.

During certain occasions, your attention may somehow be drawn to the memories, but you can control what occupies your mind. Don't spend time thinking about the things you can't change, like how long your sentence was and other people's perceptions, or your horrible encounters in jail, because such memories are disempowering. Instead, focus on the things you can count on to make you happy, like the excellent progress you have achieved up to now. That's the most rewarding option you can choose in any situation.

Since you've listed your goals, focus on what you want first, before you make plans on how to get it.

Everything can be achieved if you set your mind, heart, and soul to it. As soon as you start your journey to make great achievements, use your creativity to invent your own opportunities. You can choose to wait for opportunities. Or you can go out there and create your own. It's more empowering when you choose the latter. You will accomplish more even before you take advantage of the opportunities offered by your community.

In everything you do, let go of people's expectations. Don't be obsessed with gaining a certain status, fame, wealth, or material possessions. These are not the most important things in life. Your well-being and happiness are what you should be keen on. Let your mind be fixed on growing and living life to the fullest. Additionally, let go of relationships that do not grow you. They include negative and dishonest people, people who have no respect for you, and people who are always critical, trying to find a fault in you. They don't deserve your time.

Dedicate more of your time to people who empower you. Spend time with people you are compatible with, like-minded people who are positive, prosperous, successful, and can influence your growth. If their intentions are to help you retain a good outlook, those are the people you need most.

Aim to choose actions that nurture self-respect. This boosts confidence, and confidence is essential for achieving your goals. Taking good care of your health increases productivity and motivation. Eventually, all of this will elevate your sense of self-worth and confidence. Confidence is a strong quality that stirs up strength and courage, which are necessary for achieving what you desire in your life.

You can strengthen your character by challenging yourself to do things that other people might view as difficult. You can also use that strength to make more positive changes in your life. This strategy of developing inner strength is required to ensure that you are committed to personal growth.

It takes bravery and confidence to create the life you desire. As you learn more and value what you ultimately hope for in the future, you'll find that it means raising new standards and making significant life changes. Avoid giving in to fear of failure. It can stop you from acting.

Remember that if you don't try anything, you'll never achieve what you've planned. In fact, falling and encountering failure when you first try can be a good way to learn important lessons. For example, successful entrepreneurs discover the importance of failing as quickly as possible when endeavoring to launch a new venture. The faster you find difficulties and bugs, the faster you can eliminate them completely to make way for success.

Failing is the worst thing that could happen before you enjoy a complete transition, but you shouldn't allow it to dictate how you react, get back up again, and start living your best life.

Soon as you're up again, devote yourself to solidifying your strengths. Every strength you've been endowed with is a key to unlocking a life of excellence. Therefore, make the best use of your strengths, and you'll get to your destiny in due time.

On your way, you can learn to embrace happiness and maintain inner peace by incorporating good traits and qualities into your life. Honesty, calmness, confidence, humility, and respect are some of the essential qualities you should nurture. You might have lost your good character traits because of incarceration, but since you're now free, it's best to regain them. The time you spent locked up shouldn't change who you are negatively. It shouldn't take away your admirable qualities. It should only provoke you to emerge as an amazing person, one who can be a respectable figure in the community.

The more respect you gain, the humbler you should remain, respecting others as well. Respect keeps you on top because people know you can never be proud even if you prosper more than they do. And once you gain prosperity, you will be able to sustain it, since you haven't given in to pride that leads to a downfall. Your humility will help you maintain a successful, distinguished status.

# 30-DAY JOURNEY

The ultimate strategy for transition is comprehensively detailed in the following day-to-day plans. By the end of the thirtieth day, you will have fully adjusted to a new life. Adjusting to normalcy is a process. Depending on the length of your term, how quickly you adjust will be different compared to other ex-prisoners. The hard work you put in does matter. The steps you take to return to a normal life also play a great role.

The following thirty-day nuggets will clearly guide you on your path to a more fulfilling life after incarceration.

# FACING THE REALITY

## Day One:

## Fear Factor

Once you have been released from prison, your first and most natural reaction is FEAR. When fear fills you, it doesn't mean you're a coward. You're not a failure, either. It means you're normal, that you're reacting to change. This reaction is totally okay. Take it calmly without beating yourself up for it. It's natural. And because you had been anticipating your release for a while, the realization that change is coming soon makes fear more evident.

Everything you want is on the other side of fear. The excellence, the prosperity, the wealth, the ideal job; and the happiness you've so much longed for can be found once you march right through fear without letting it have authority over you. Despite the extremity of your fear, you can conquer it if you believe in yourself. It doesn't matter how long you've been free. What's significant is your faith and your strong will. These two possessions give you the strength to fight fear. They make you discover how the potential in you is greater than the fear that has been holding you. When you correctly use that potential, fear will start going away. It may not disappear immediately, but soon it will no longer have a devastating effect on you.

During the time you're most vulnerable, it can be difficult to fight fear. The first few days after you step out of prison are the most challenging. That's the time you need the most support. If your family and friends stand by you at this time, it will be easier to face your fear and eventually overcome it. When you're finally free, and you find someone who is concerned and willing to help you make it through, accept their help.

The best thing you can have as you go through a transition is someone to talk to. It becomes easier to overcome fear when you speak out what's troubling you and your thoughts about the future.

As you talk it out, you'll discover that the difficulties you thought would break you won't seem that tough anymore. The fact is, no matter how tough your situation seems, it can be dealt with if you don't let fear hold you down. You're probably asking how you'll conquer it, after the difficult period you went through in prison.

First, let your mind be free from thoughts of isolation, or the loneliness you faced in jail. Affirm that you're going out to a world of people who want to help you get back your life. Avoid the temptation of carrying that weight all by yourself. Let those who care to, be there for you. If you allow them to hold your hand, loneliness will not check in. Neither will isolation, both of which cause fear.

When you have people who care around you, fear that something bad might happen will not torture you either. The apprehension caused by the fear of going to an unknown future will drift away because you'll find out that with good assistance all around you, no mountains are unmovable.

# Day Two:

# Avoid Triggers

Everyone has triggers or little things that cause them to react embarrassingly or without thinking at times. A trigger is anything that causes you to react to situations in a bad way; something that causes you to feel upset and frightened because it makes you remember a bad event which happened in the past.

A trigger sparks off a flashback, taking your mind back to a traumatic event. It could be an unpleasant memory, a photo, or a song. Whatever your trigger is, identify it. Then make it a priority to alleviate its impact on you. Even if sometimes it's difficult to erase bad memories out of your mind, you have the power to control what those memories make you feel. Once you realize the memories and the trauma are in the past, you will give them less attention and eventually eliminate them from your mind.

The biggest challenge is learning how to deal with triggers effectively. Studies show that those who relapse often did so as a result of a trigger. But when you use the power that you must to resist the effects of a trigger, you won't be among those who relapse.

You can only overcome triggers if you acknowledge that you have them. Then, take the time to analyze them. Examine what really goes on when you react wrongly. If negative emotions like bitterness or anger get the better of you, try to suppress them when a tough situation arises. It's normal to feel angry when someone provokes you, but how you handle it determines how strong you are. Act wisely, by controlling extreme reactions. Let calmness take over regardless of what's happening around you.

One way to effectively handle triggers is to be careful where most of your energy goes. If you often find yourself getting caught up in fixes, brawls, and arguments, you should stop for a minute and reexamine what grabs your attention, your energy, and your time. The more you let yourself dwell on risky situations, the more some trigger is likely to provoke you.

Other triggers could be the environment you're living in or the places you often visited before incarceration. While it may not be possible to relocate to a better place, gather your strength whenever you pass by places that evoke terrible feelings or memories. Tell yourself that nothing can affect you anymore.

Perhaps you might pass by your old office and remember a work-related confrontation. Or you could pass by a club you used to visit and remember a fight or a shooting. Whenever such memories hit you as you pass by a place, don't run away. Stand still, face them, confess how much stronger you are—and keep walking with confidence.

## Day Three:

## Don't Go at It Alone

You're free now, and you're going to a world which is continually developing. New advancements might have come up when you were still incarcerated. If your sentence was long, you might find it hard to catch up with everything that has been going on. It could overwhelm you. That's why you need a mentor.

Mentoring is the perfect way to keep your head in the game. Someone who is more knowledgeable than you will give you the correct guidance, to help you make the best decisions as you start afresh. They will guide you on how to choose the most suitable direction. Starting from the profession you're interested in, to the skills you need to gain and how to interact with people, a mentor will take every step with you. They will stop you just in time before you make a mistake.

Therefore, find a mentor who is committed to helping you during your first steps on the journey to recovery, because these first steps are the most important. They can make or break you. By listening to the advice of a mentor, you avoid the mistakes that could stop your progress.

# Day Four:

# Leverage Resources

Although you're just getting out, remember the community is ready to support you. They'd like to see a positive, magnificent transformation in your life. There are plenty of resources you can take advantage of. From programs to jobs, your community is equipped to handle your basic and most practical request.

All you need to do is take the chance. Don't be embarrassed about your previous life. Tell them what you envision in the new life you're beginning. They will support your vision in any way they can. Accept what the community is offering, knowing that these resources can amazingly elevate your quality of life. Some of the programs include employment opportunities, depending on the skills you have. And if you don't have any skills yet, there are learning programs specially designed for people like you. Through these learning programs, you can acquire communication skills, social skills, writing skills, and even artistic skills.

Any initiative that your community has organized to help you out, don't let it pass you by. Let it be something that improves your life, something that takes you a step further as you reach out for success.

# Day Five:

## Patience

It's wise to understand that in order to realize a successful transition, you must be patient. It takes patience and perseverance to change your life successfully. In every area of your life, you must allow patience so that you can be effective. Everything in your life requires you to take it one step at a time without rushing.

It's possible you could become impatient when you see how other ex-prisoners have transitioned faster than you. Their speed is their own. Move at your own pace. This is because it would be devastating to experience a milestone you were not ready for at the time. For example, if you had anticipated becoming a public speaker, it would be essential to get psychological help first, together with social and communication skills. Otherwise, it would be heartbreaking for you to rush into public speaking, only for you to break down in front of your audience. You don't want to go through this kind of embarrassment, so be patient with yourself, even if it means waiting for months after you're released.

And because you'll have outlined your goals, be patient as you take steps to achieve them. It could be months. Long-term goals can even take years to accomplish. Nevertheless, don't give them up because of the seemingly long time you're supposed to work your way up. If you look at it from a reasonable perspective, you really need a lot of time to accomplish long-term goals. Whether it's breaking an addiction, going to university, breaking a bad habit, or owning a home; be kind to yourself and take all the time you need. That doesn't mean you're wasting time. It means you're using time—which is one of the greatest resources—to make your dreams come to reality successfully.

# Day Six:

# Evaluate New Friendships and Every Family Member

Now that you are back home, old friends will want to acquaint themselves. At this point, you should be extremely careful who you allow back in your life. What are their intentions? Some of them just want to hear what you went through then use it against you later. Avoid opening up to everyone so quickly. You need friends, but you don't need those with bad intentions. Take your time before you let anyone in. If you follow your instincts, you will recognize those who really want the best for you.

Whenever someone is getting close to you suddenly, be extremely cautious. Their aim could be to bring you down again since not everyone is happy to see you're finally free.

And whenever someone new wants to befriend you, check on their background. You don't have to know much about them to determine if they're good friends. A little information will do. Like, how do they earn a living? Who do they spend their time with? Such information can help you know if a friendship is right.

Your family members are the most important, but you should evaluate them, too. Some of them might still have a negative attitude toward you just because you were incarcerated. Their attitude shouldn't move you at all. Be firm and strong as you reconcile with them. Then give them time to see how much better you're becoming. Before you get too close to them, let them acknowledge you're wiser than you used to be. When they realize this, their attitude will change, and you can then rebuild that strong family bond.

# Day Seven:

# Plan and Prioritize

There's an old saying that states, "If you fail to plan, you plan to fail." This statement is true for every situation you're in. It's not for business-oriented people only or students. It's for everyone, and that includes you.

A week after you're released and your life is slowly coming around, you should start listing down your priorities. What's the most important thing you should shift your attention to at this moment? Is it your health? Mental health or physical health? Is it both? Or, do you need emotional support from your family?

Maybe you need to start adjusting to a new daily schedule. When you recognize your priorities, start doing something about them. Fulfill them first before you move on to something else.

In the meantime, start making plans. List the meaningful things you want to do in the coming days. Plan how you're going to spend your time. When you're not so occupied, focus on your growth. In your areas of weakness, try to find out how you can stop them from pulling you back. This will be greatly helpful because you'll avoid the mistakes that can spoil your plans.

After you face reality in the normal world you've come back to, the next step is improving yourself professionally. Your career is very important, and here are some of the ways you can steer it in the right direction.

## Day Eight:

## Invest in Yourself

Before you start your career, make a brilliant first impression. Appearance is everything. It says a lot about you even before you speak. Dress up professionally in a way you're most comfortable. Professional attire will speak volumes about the new you. It will show how determined you are to succeed in your career, and how much you value the impression you make.

Investing in yourself physically, spiritually, emotionally, and financially will empower you to become the best version of yourself. As a result, you will be a role model and an inspiration to others. They will become interested in knowing how you've wonderfully evolved to be better than anyone would expect. Some of those who will admire you have probably been locked up before, so don't hesitate to give them advice. Your advice will save their lives, and they will remember you years later when their lives become fully stable.

Always remember that the value and potential you possess is significant and enough for you. It can make you achieve incredible success. Therefore, give it the time, opportunity, and energy to grow and bring results. The results are a good life full of hope and abundance. You will never lack what you need if you fully use your potential. You'll have more than enough; more to give to those who will need it when their time comes.

When you think about investing in yourself, everything that you possess matters: your health, your confidence, your spirituality, your emotions, and your creativity. The most rewarding investment is one that's entirely about you. It means that everything you are is excellently taken care of, and when that's done, you are adequately empowered to possess prosperity, wealth, and success.

# Day Nine:

## Build a Support System

Once you have identified your goal and a potential opportunity, it's now time to attach yourself to the right people. Surround yourself with smart people who can help you reach your goals. Most likely, they specialize in the same profession you're planning to pursue. They know a lot about it—the ups, the downs, the qualities you're supposed to adopt if you want to make it. Open your mind and listen to their wisdom. Be ready to learn new things as you count on their support.

This right attitude helps you boost your creativity and your expertise. What you already know is not enough to accelerate a breakthrough. If you only rely on your own knowledge, it will take longer for you to reach that milepost. Take a moment to listen to the advice of those who support you. Sometimes it can mean changing your plans so that you can properly follow their advice. Alter your plans if you must, because they may not work best at that time.

When the right people stand with you while you endeavor to actualize your goal, success is guaranteed.

## Day Ten:

## Opportunities

You now have support, and that means multiple opportunities will come knocking at your door. Before you open it, ask yourself: what's my goal? Do I want to start a business, go back to school, or take up a trade?

A world of opportunities awaits. Choosing the most favorable ones can be difficult. There's no reason to struggle with that difficulty, though. Grab the opportunities that align with your goals. They will work best for you. They will be the most profitable and yield greater results because that's where you'll find the biggest accomplishment. It will even get better when you pursue realistic goals that can be achieved within the current opportunities. Everything will work for you, and you won't struggle on your way up.

# Day Eleven:

# Strategy

Drawing up a good strategy will help you stay focused and provide a definitive tool to help close the gap. You'll be able to make up for the time you spent in jail, and the opportunities you lost.

A good strategy is one that favors you in the state you're currently in. For instance, you might still be recovering from depression. At the same time, you'd like to start your new career. How can you successfully manage to achieve both goals? You take it easy at first. Until you recover completely, don't push yourself too hard at the workplace. Take breaks and days off when you should. Complete your counseling and therapy sessions. If you're on medication, take everything the doctor has prescribed at the right time.

The same applies to every other goal you might have—business goals, education goals, family, and relationship goals. Adopt a patient but effective approach. Never force anything to happen. If you're playing your part, let things fall into place at the appropriate time. Your role is to write up a plan that shows how you plan to get things together. Then, specify when you'd like to achieve this, and the period you'll need. This plan accelerates your pace, while you're still taking it one day at a time.

It's rewarding to have a strategy because it will facilitate the realization of your purpose, which will, in turn, make your life more meaningful.

## Day Twelve:

## Execute

You are responsible for your own success. You might have support from family, friends, and mentors, but in the end, succeeding depends entirely on you. Your actions determine the extent of your success.

Your attitude contributes, too. Along the way, there will be discouragement, but that—and any other negative element—shouldn't spoil your attitude. Keep your spirits high because every discouragement will pass. No opposition can pull you down if you have a positive attitude. You will override all opposing elements because you're busy executing the strategy you've already written down.

Executing your strategy involves following the rules that propel you to achievement. Be consistent as you stick to the rules, and everything you listed in your plan will come true. Inconsistency pulls you a step backward, so as you abide by the rules, resist everything that threatens to spoil the rhythm. Bad tendencies, wrong judgment, and stubbornness can destroy your progress, so get over them and maintain your pace.

**Day Thirteen:**

**Communicate and Follow Up**

Communication is key. It facilitates your progress day after day. As you approach two weeks of freedom, you will have learned better communication skills. The way you used to interact with inmates and correctional officers is not the same way you will interact with your family, friends, and colleagues. The good thing about communication is that you learn about it on the go. When you talk to people, you will instinctively know how to make yourself heard in the right manner. Learn to listen while you're at it. Excellent communication involves listening, giving the other person a chance to express themselves.

They will do the same for you, and when they do, speak up as clearly as you can. Be polite, too. Express your thoughts and feelings precisely, so that you can get help when you need it. You will eventually learn the art of great communication as your life improves.

Avoid holding back ideas or thoughts you feel you need to speak up. They will exert a heavy weight on you if you keep them to yourself. When you talk and participate in discussions, you help bring solutions to the problem at hand. Others benefit from your idea, and when you need their suggestions, they will readily share with you. Therefore, good communication eases your integration to the community, and your whole life as well. It takes the pressure off you since you have the confidence to speak up and confide in someone when you need to.

## Day Fourteen:
## Be Persistent

In your effort to maintain consistent growth, be respectful, yet ask questions. You are in the process of learning, and the best way to learn is to ask questions where you don't understand. Sometimes when you ask, you might get *no* as an answer. It's important to remain calm and respectful. Try to understand why they said no; or why you haven't gotten the desired response that relates to your goal.

The main reason why you didn't get the answer you expected is that your perspective changed the moment you were incarcerated. Most likely, the way you looked at things became entirely different. And because you hadn't realized how much your perspective had changed, you hoped everything would go like you expected it to. There was frustration when they said no, perhaps no to your request for a job, financial assistance, or anything else. However, don't let that discourage you.

Keep on being persistent, because in the process, you will learn what's right, and you'll be able to let go of your flawed outlook. Furthermore, perseverance brings hope. It keeps you assured that if you hold on, something good will come out of all this, and the lessons you've learned will make you a more valuable person.

In your personal life, there are several things you'll have to acknowledge, to ease your transition. More effort is required when it comes to your personal life. Although you'll look for assistance, you have the greatest role to play to accelerate the advancement of your personal life.

## Day Fifteen:
## Expect Setbacks

Since you've now completed two weeks of freedom, setbacks are likely to come your way as you return to normalcy. They shouldn't catch you by surprise, because if they do, they might interfere with your transition.

Right from the day you're released, expect challenges at certain points in your progress. Most of the time, setbacks come up just when you're about to move a step further. During such moments, hold on to your potential. You have the potential to beat every setback that pops up along the way. Let it build you instead of crush you. Let it be a stepping-stone to a higher level in your personality, your relationships, your career, and your wellness.

Whenever a setback shows up, counter its effects with the right mindset, and solutions that facilitate a breakthrough. You cannot allow difficulties to change your mind at this point. You're the one who can change the effects setbacks have on you. Let them make you a wiser, stronger, and more resourceful person.

## Day Sixteen:

## Balance Your Life

Once you've started adjusting to a free life, it's natural to get excited about what the real world holds.

This excitement can make you concentrate more on certain things and neglect others. As much as you want to live your new life to the fullest, you must divide your attention to all the important areas in your life.

Living a well-balanced life isn't just essential for your health, peace, and wellness, it's also important for increasing productivity, maintaining your happiness, and unleashing your greatest potential.

Every day when you're continuously attempting to move forward with your purpose and to achieve your goals, you should strive to take care of the different elements of your life, balancing them all the while. These include your health, your spiritual alignment, your relationships, and your career

Whenever any aspect of your life takes away a disproportionate amount of energy, you tend to shortchange the other aspects. That throws you off, making you unable to move forward on life's tightrope until you reestablish a balance. Make it a priority to deal with any areas that are taking too much energy.

Avoid letting them drain you by putting them on the spot, aligning them, and balancing them so that you can preserve energy for all other areas.

There are simple things you can do to get back your balance. Reward yourself with a break: Take some time off to unwind. Let the tension and anxiety go while you relax and recharge. It could be a few hours a day or during the weekends. Turn off your laptops and smartphones and do something engaging. Explore hobbies that boost the positive energy inside you. Talk to someone you love, read an interesting book, go for a gym session, or meditate. Such relaxing activities take your mind away from the tension and anxiety that causes you to neglect important areas in your life.

When you attain this balance, you'll be more productive in your career. You'll have more power to implement your strategies, chase after your dreams, and work toward achieving your goals.

## Day Seventeen:

## Deal with Your Issues

Soon after you're set free, personal issues will be inevitable. You might experience problems with your emotions, how you relate to the people around you, how you handle your finances, and how you stick to your daily schedule. The first several days will be challenging, but extra perseverance will get you through.

If you want to get rid of your issues, you must take a practical course of action. Do things in a different and better way. Although you cannot solve problems unless you confront them, you must confront them in a different way. This means changing your approach. Redirect your thinking. Stop relying on the same suggestions that didn't work out the last time. There's always a better, alternative way to resolve issues, so be open to it and get into action.

Finding solutions starts with admitting that you have a problem that you can't solve immediately. Your situation might seem difficult, but that doesn't mean you can never solve your problems. It just requires some extra effort. Making extra effort means you'll have to make sacrifices at various points in your life.

The sacrifices you make could cost you a little more dedication and energy, but if you know the breakthrough you're about to celebrate, you'll find that the sacrifice was worth it.

After you deal with your issues and they are out of the way, you will create a clear channel to allow help, which you need most at this time.

**Day Eighteen:**

**Ask for Help**

Sometimes, help doesn't just come automatically. You must ask for it. The first requirement is acknowledging you can't fix everything all by yourself. Struggling to do so would completely deplete your strength. You need help from someone stronger, wiser, and more experienced than you. They have wisdom and are more insightful than you, so their assistance will mean so much to you. You may not realize this immediately, but as you move forward in your new life, you will notice the benefits of the help you asked for.

Always be polite as you seek assistance. This will make people respect you and want to offer a helping hand even before you tell them what your problem is.

# Day Nineteen:

# Look at Yourself

Take some time to assess how much you have grown. Has your personality changed? Has it changed for the better, or taken a turn for the worse? If it has become better, you are on the right path. But if you haven't been able to adjust to the new life, you need extra help and persistence.

First, identify what has been holding you back. Is it a personal weakness, or failure to fully embrace change? Write down what has been your biggest obstacle. Once you recognize it, you'll be in an advantageous position where you can address it and amplify your strengths. Strengthening your potential makes you get through difficult times. That's why self-assessment is very crucial at this stage where you need to keep moving.

Your strengths will facilitate your growth despite your current environment or circumstances. The evidence that you're still moving motivates you to press on. Your weaknesses won't trouble you anymore because you've already analyzed them and found a way to conquer them.

**Day Twenty:**

# Identify the Gaps

You've dealt with your issues, and it's now appropriate to look for the unfilled gaps in your life. This includes your personal life, profession, and all types of relationships. Find out what needs more attention, then search for a way to suitably fill that gap.

Maybe when you were jailed, your role in the family couldn't be played by anyone else, and that left a heavy burden on them. Since you're back now, do your best to make up for those times you should have been there for them. Do a little more than you usually did before incarceration. Dedicate more of your time to your family and your career. As you do this, remember to maintain the balance. Resultantly, you'll fill the gap and probably achieve more than you would have anticipated before you went to jail.

# Day Twenty-one:

## Reinvent or Improve Where Necessary

Reinvention is an endless process, always happening as you live every day. The decisions you make during this process are very significant. They determine whether you're moving forward or backward. A successful reinvention happens when you start afresh completely. Your previous life, reputation, fame, or job should have nothing to do with the new life you're starting.

In the course of your reinvention, do what you love best. It doesn't have to be approved by other people or match their passion. Keep on doing what you enjoy, and you will be successful. Meanwhile, identify who you should connect with and talk to. The right connections increase your chances of succeeding, so examine the network you've established. The connections in your life should favor your growth as well as your reinvention.

In case you've already made remarkable progress, try to make improvements where you can. Let your quest for reinvention inspire you to advance more. With time, your growth will be a continuous process that makes you stand out and gain positive recognition wherever you go.

# Day Twenty-two:

# Say No

You don't have to accept everything people tell you. Some opinions and suggestions can be misleading. You might have spent years in prison, and it would be tempting to believe what everyone says. But you don't have to. Learn to say no to misleading viewpoints.

You might sometimes have a hard time saying no because you haven't taken the time to evaluate their relationships and recognize your part in the relationship. After you clearly understand how you interact in the relationship and your role in it, you won't be troubled about the results that come with saying no. You'll realize that your relationship is strong and can withstand your firm answer.

Being unable to say no can make you tensed up, tired, stressed out, and irritable. It could be undermining any dedication you make to advance your quality of life. Worse still, you might spend hours worrying about getting out of a previously promised commitment.

To avoid unnecessary worry, always stay true to yourself. Be sincere and honest with yourself about what you really want. As you enjoy your freedom, learn to know yourself better. You can do this by refocusing on what you really want from life.

Remain firm, despite who—or what—you've said no to. If someone can't accept the reality that you are saying "no," then you should know they are probably not a true friend. They may even not respect you. Stand your ground, and don't feel compelled to say yes just because that person is disappointed.

# Day Twenty-three:

# Have Faith

Faith can completely heal your life. Have faith in God and in yourself. He has held your hand all the while, and if you stay firm in your faith, you will move levels higher. Let your confidence in Him and in yourself never end. It will help you overcome limits you thought would hinder your progress. Unwavering confidence and faith make the seemingly insurmountable mountains move.

Your transition is not just about you. It's about leaving a positive imprint in your community, too. The help you got came from your community, and you should show your gratitude by doing everything in your power to make an outstanding contribution.

Here are ways to make this possible:

# Day Twenty-four:

# Pursue Your Purpose

By this time, you've discovered your purpose, what you were really meant to be. Be relentless in your pursuit. You've learned how to override setbacks, and all you can expect now is winning. Living your purpose brings prosperity since you'll be experiencing the life that was meant for you from the very beginning.

For you to make your purpose established, you should discover who you are first. The jail term you served shouldn't define who you are, whether it took years, months, or days. Your gifts, your personality, and your potential make up the real you. Your experiences only make you wiser and stronger. After you discover yourself, keep what you want to achieve in mind, then find out what you need in order to achieve it. The resources in your community are the major things you need to realize your purpose. Make the most of them, because they're there to help you reach the next milestone.

Your breakthrough not only helps you; it benefits your family and your community.

# Day Twenty-five:

# An Act of Kindness

All these days, you've been helped along the way. You wouldn't have come this far if you embarked on this journey alone. Since your life is finally coming together, go out of your way, and extend generosity and kindness to others.

It takes a simple act of doing good—you don't have to be rich to show generosity. The little you can do will go a long way. There are many things you can do to show kindness. Visit the elderly, donate to children's homes, help in the event of natural disasters, give advice to young people who are just starting out in life, or organize a get-together party for your family. Do anything that you can do to show other people you care about them. In the long run, you'll feel accomplished because you brought a smile to someone's face.

# Day Twenty-six:

# Stay Motivated

From time to time, seek inspiration that provokes you to desire to keep going, regardless of your environment or your situation. Everything may not be perfect yet, but you need to keep your hopes high. A good source of motivation every day will help you remain steadfast. It will inspire you to put more effort in your pursuit of success.

Hope will make you realize that your hard work is not in vain. A reward awaits you at the finish line. That reward is peace, tranquility, greatness, prosperity, and wealth.

# Day Twenty-seven:

## Make a Difference in the Lives of Others

Because you've followed the advice given in this book, you now have the capacity to be a role model. You can make a remarkable, impactful change in your community, and even in your country. Use your wisdom to influence others positively. Let your talents benefit them, as they prosper you more.

The way you speak and act should be of good impact to others. Your words should build someone instead of breaking— everything you do also matters. Your actions alone can positively transform someone's life.

## Day Twenty-eight:

## Continue to Give Back

By this time, success will start becoming evident in your life. You've begun making it. Don't give pride a chance. Continue to be kind. Keep on doing good deeds. Whenever you can, take part in charitable projects in your community. Don't be tired of giving back. Make it something you occasionally do for the rest of your life. When you give back, more prosperity comes your way. A greater sense of accomplishment and fulfillment fills you, and the emptiness you felt because of your incarceration goes away.

## Day Twenty-nine:

## Reward Yourself from Time to Time

Every time you accomplish a goal, motivate yourself in a bigger way by rewarding yourself. Whenever you overcome a bad habit, congratulate yourself for it, and treat yourself to the things you love. Your reward should give you the enthusiasm to maintain the better personality you're adopting. When you maintain your progress, you can be sure you'll never go back—you can only win, and your victory will last.

# Day Thirty:

## Tell Your Story Over and Over

What you encountered before, during, and after incarceration shouldn't be an embarrassment to you any longer. It should be a story that changes your life and the lives of others. Your story can rescue someone who was on the verge of committing a crime. It can stop them from making the same mistake you made, so tell it many times, whenever you see someone who needs to hear it. Those who become transformed by hearing your story will be thankful that someone stepped in just in time. Share your experience with young people who are most likely to break the law due to certain difficulties in life.

Young people need your story more than anyone else. Recount it as many times as you can, telling them how you kept your faith and eventually overcame.

# ABOUT THE AUTHOR

Malcolm Allen is a recognized expert on human potential and (BCSA) Board Certified Social Advocate. He migrates effortlessly between corporate boardrooms and underserved communities aiming to advance the interests of social justice, particularly on behalf of populations or groups who have been disadvantaged, disempowered, or forgotten.

Allen has authored over two dozen books, and most have achieved best-selling status. He has worked with subject matter experts and credentialed instruction designers to socially engineer a platform of outcome-based programs that provide solutions for disabled veterans, recidivism, human trafficking, dropout prevention, bullying, diversity, mentoring, financial inclusion, entrepreneurship, and leadership. All programs are Military Approved, and available at Penn Foster College and Graduate America Centers of Excellence around the world. For seminar licensing, book purchases, or speaker requests, please visit: <u>Unconditional.org</u>